Bernard Lievegoed

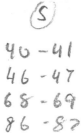

40 - 41
46 - 47
68 - 69
86 - 87

The Eye of the Needle

His life and working encounter
with anthroposophy

An interview with Jelle van der Meulen

Translated by Philip Mees

Hawthorn Press

Translated from the Dutch, *Het oog van de naald*, by
Bernard Lievegoed MD

UCC Copyright notice: © 1991 Uitgeverij Vrij
Geestesleven, Zeist, Holland.
English edition: © 1993 Hawthorn Press, Hawthorn
House, 1 Lansdown Lane, Stroud, Glos. GL5 1BJ UK

Typeset in Plantin by Saxon Graphics, Derby, UK.
Printed by The Cromwell Press, Broughton Gifford.

A catalogue recording of this book is available from the
British Library
ISBN 1 869 89050 7

TABLE OF CONTENTS

Foreword

We spoke with each other for three days, one day in his vacation house in the lake country in Friesland, two days in his study in Zeist. The conversations did not only take us to the most important events of the difficult century that almost lies behind us but also to the future. For that is what Bernard Lievegoed always aims at, even when he speaks about the past: the things that are to come. Also now that he has reached the age of 85 years he seems to consider everything he says as preparation for tomorrow.

Bernard Lievegoed is an anthroposophist. His whole life carries the stamp of the practical application of the spiritual science introduced by Rudolf Steiner between 1900 and 1925. In a certain sense you could say that, from the nineteen thirties on, the course of Bernard Lievegoed's life coincides with the development of the anthroposophical movement in the Netherlands. Many of the questions he has struggled with over the decades are questions that characterize the development of this movement.

But besides being an anthroposophist, Bernard Lievegoed is also a 'contemporary', i.e. the great changes western civilization went through since the nineteen thirties left their mark on his life and work. The important themes of his fruitful life are all derived from the needs of his time.

The conversations in this book take the reader not only into Lievegoed's study but also into his inner room. Lievegoed himself calls the reality of this inner room his 'inner biography', as opposed to his 'outer biography'. The fact that, after some understandable hesitation, he speaks freely in this

5

book about his inner side undoubtedly has to do with the awareness that no exterior can be understood without its interior. And this, besides his orientation to the future, is a second essential characteristic of Bernard Lievegoed: his acting on the basis of inner (esoteric) motives.

Bernard Lievegoed is an esotericist, however, not in the sense of the 'mysterious' or 'cryptic'. Anyone who has had something to do with anthroposophists or anthroposophical organizations will know that there is often a gap between the visible foreground and the invisible background. What anthroposophists *do* (in Waldorf schools, in bio-dynamic agriculture, in medicine) is often experienced as sensible and refreshing but what they *think* remains dim and unintelligible.

Bernard Lievegoed often succeeds in bridging that gap. Also in his speaking and writing about the esoteric background, his boldness shows itself. To him, the fear of being misunderstood is simply not there. He says what he has to say, in his own manner, at moments that seem right to him. In this sense, he is a modern esotericist who, with conviction and without timidity, places the contents of spiritual science in the bright light of public life. That this attitude often generated conflicts, especially in the anthroposophical movement, will not be surprising. That aspect of Lievegoed's life also comes to the fore in these conversations.

Bernard Lievegoed wants to realize anthroposophy. That explains the many institutions he has founded, such as the institute for curative education 'Zonnehuizen Veldheim/Stenia', the NPI – Instituut voor Organisatie Ontwikkeling[1], and the Vrije Hogeschool[2]. That also

---

[1]NPI – Institute for Organizational Development
[2]The Vrije Hogeschool is a one year course for students preparing for university.

6

explains his work at universities and the many books he published, such as *The Developing Organization, Man on the Threshold*, and his recent book *Mensheidsperspectiven*.[3] Both the books and the institutions are meant to serve everyone, not just anthroposophists.

I *wanted* these conversations with Bernard Lievegoed. The reason I wanted them lay in some questions I had been living with for a longer period of time. Some of these questions relate to Bernard Lievegoed as a person; after reading this book, the reader will no doubt understand what questions I mean. Other questions have to do with the role the anthroposophical society has played in this century and could play in the coming time. Because I knew Lievegoed as someone who lives with the same questions I felt I could invite him for these conversations.

But Lievegoed would not have been Lievegoed if he had not attached a very specific condition to his consent to the conversation. There are, he said, a few urgent themes he wanted to bring out because they are important for the coming time. In brief, he wanted to talk about the future. During the conversations, however, it became clear that these themes were connected with my questions, so we did not need to be in each other's way.

In the last chapter, Bernard Lievegoed takes over the initiative. There he has recorded what he wanted to say himself. However, the reader will find that the first three chapters, which are based on my questions, anticipate the fourth.

A few days after I had sent him the manuscript for his review I received it back with a few suggestions in the margins for amplifications. To my surprise he had crossed

---

[3]*Mensheidsperspectieven* is not available in English. Translated, the title reads: *Perspectives of Mankind*.
The bibliography includes a list of Bernard Lievegoed's books and the other books referred to in the text.

hardly anything out, but had only made additions. Without exception, these additions have been incorporated in the text. The big surprise was, however, that on the last sheets he had added a brief, pencil written summary which can be seen as a kind of 'afterword', a recapitulation of the conversation that shows what for him are the main points. This addition has been incorporated in the book under the title 'Afterword'.

This book is not a biographical sketch, although the future biographer – certain to come at some time – will find much useful material in it. It came about from Lievegoed's willingness to talk about his life and from my wondering about all he does in his life. The text can best be seen as a story in which the lead character is not just the lead but also the narrator of the story.

Jelle van der Meulen
Amsterdam, 1991

I. Youth in the Dutch East Indies

Bernard Lievegoed's parents leave Holland for the island of Sumatra, Indonesia (formerly the Dutch East Indies) in 1902 (the father) and 1903 (the mother), where the father becomes editor of the *Sumatra Post*. On September 2, 1905, Bernard is born in Medan, Sumatra. There he goes to grade school, takes frequent hikes in the mountains and makes friends with contemporaries from a variety of religions. After a two year stay in Rotterdam, Holland, he comes to Java in his twelfth year. There, his father becomes editor in chief of *The Locomotive*, the largest newspaper in the Dutch East Indies. On Java, Bernard completes high school. He passes his final pre-university exams in 1923 in The Hague.

'He is rich because he has many relationships.'

Bernard Lievegoed: 'Growing up on Sumatra and Java, that means undergoing the overwhelming power of nature. With my friends, I often set out on Sundays at five in the morning with our guns, shooting fish in the Semarang river. At first dawn, they would come to the surface to get air. Of course, it was a rare day when we actually hit one. But if you did, you thought that was tremendous. When unexpectedly you did hit one you gave a nickel to a little Javanese boy who would then dive into the water and retrieve the fish for you.

Also, we often went to the place in the river where the praos were moored. During the week, these were used to get sand from the shoals for the building trade. On Sundays, they were tied up with chains and locks you could open with a crooked nail. So we borrowed the prao from the guard and went all four of us into the river to the shoals shooting alligators! If you happened to hit one it would immediately slither into the water and you had lost it. And yet, we thought we did useful work. The Javanese had a fair amount of trouble with these animals because in the middle of the night they would come onto the land and steal chickens from their coops.

During these expeditions we only wore straw hats, otherwise we were fully naked. Because there were so many rapids, you had to get in the water all the time to pull and guide the boat through the many narrow passages. Five hours and a lot of rapids later you came to a higher area where most of the time we made a fire, cooked some rice, and shot birds of prey. On Java you had some curious customs: the local youth shot pigeons and we shot birds of prey. Towards the end of the afternoon, we went back again, but now with the current. The trick was then to steer the boat with long sticks through the wild rapids. Within an hour we were back in Semarang.

Then you had the big mountain hikes. When it was vacation time we rented a little house on the slope of the Merbabu which is about 10,000 feet high: one of those little Javanese houses of woven mats and a roof of palm leaves. From there we made trips. We always left in the evening because it is better to climb in the cool air. The next day we would arrive at the top very early in the morning. The view there . . . everywhere around you mountain peaks, and down below a sea of clouds. On the top of that mountain lived a hermit who would sell you a cup of coffee for two and a half cents. He got the water somewhere from a spring.

During the day, we slept up there, and toward the evening we started the descent along the other side of the mountain to the summer palace of the Sultan of Solo. When he was not there you could stay there, that is, if you gave the guards some money. Then you got assigned to one of the women's quarters. There was a toilet there with at least fifteen holes next to each other above the river. There we would sit, all together, and talk. Going to the toilet was a social happening there. Behind the Merbabu was a second mountain, the Merapi, an active volcano you could not always climb because of the sulphuric fumes. With the wind behind you, it was possible to descend into the crater. On the bottom there was a plug of rubble from which wisps of smoke rose up.

Such trips would take about five days. Towards the evening, we would go to a village and ask the *lura*, the village chief, if we could spend the night there. Around a small oil lamp, we would hear endless stories about the harvest, the events in the village, and about who was poor and who was rich. Wealth is very different there from how it is here in the West. I remember someone telling me about a man who was very rich. I asked, what do you mean rich, does he have a lot of money? No, the man didn't have money. Then does he own a lot of land? No, of course he owned no land either. Well, what does he have? The answer was: the man is rich because he has many relationships.

Actually, the Javanese word for "rich" that was used here cannot be easily translated. I asked if I could meet this man and the next morning I was taken to a small house. The man was sitting on the floor plaiting strands of bamboo for repairs to his house. I said to the lura: what's so unusual about this man? This man, was the answer, has helped many people!

Later I understood what was meant. In this Javanese community you are considered rich when you have helped many people. For, if you have helped many other people you have the right to say to them: come and help me repair

11

my house, I also helped you at one time. When you use such help the debt is paid off. But if you leave the debt standing you have people everywhere who have to help you when you really need it. The Javanese say the more you give away the richer you become.'

Were you interested in the differences between western and Javanese culture?
'I wanted to understand the Javanese culture. I also wanted to know what the Javanese thought about us Westerners. Next to our vacation house lived the assistant head of the regional administration. He had a son who one day graduated from the technical high school in Surabaya. That was celebrated with festivities that lasted for a week. Wayang dancers played scenes from the Hindu epic Mahabharata from six in the evening to six in the morning, seven days in a row. For hours and hours, the Javanese sat there squatting in a circle. They knew every detail of the stories, yet they stayed and watched and were never bored. We Westerners prefer to watch a play we have not seen before. But these Javanese were continuously absorbed by the images of the Mahabharata. That made a big impression on me.

Between the scenes of the Mahabahrata, there were intermezzos. Every time, the same two characters came on stage, a short fat one and a tall skinny one. In the play, they played a part just like Mercury in Greek mythology; they were the messengers of the gods. What an archetypal image, right? The fat one and the skinny one! In the intermission, however, they did not act as messengers of the gods, but as comedians. They would discuss all kinds of events of the village with each other. They would make the Javanese laugh a lot. I did not understand them and at one moment, when one of the two had just made some very funny movements, I asked why they had laughed so hard. I was told he had imitated the gait of a European.

Later, I asked our house boy Abdul, with whom I had a good relationship, what was so funny about Europeans. You know what it is, he said, you guys are not civilized. You guys laugh when you are not supposed to laugh, you ask questions you are not supposed to ask, and when you walk you make clumsy movements.'

You weren't insulted?
'Not in the least! I thought he was completely right! One day, our house boy Abdul (his nickname was Dul) came to my father and asked if he could have a week off to go to his village. Well, what is the matter? my father asked. You know, Dul said, my mother died and I have to bury her. My father remembered that Dul's mother had already died six months earlier and that Dul had then also asked for time off. Therefore, he said: out of the question, you don't need to bury your mother twice, do you?

No, tuan, said Abdul, that is right . . . But, asked my father, what then is the trouble? Well, said Dul, I would still like to bury my mother. OK then, my father replied, but I am disappointed that you use such lies to me. The same evening I asked Dul what the matter was and he said: you know, you guys show so little understanding. If it is so crystal clear that I am lying that means I can't tell you the real reason. Then you shouldn't ask any further. Then you are supposed to say: Dul, I hope your mother will have a good burial!'

Did you have friends among the Indonesians?
'In high school I was in a class of twenty-four students. Two of those were what you call European boys. Seven were of Chinese origin, five Javanese, and one was black. The rest

13

were Indos[4]. I shared my desk with a Chinese boy, Bee Tat Kwan, with whom I have had a very warm friendship. He came from an orthodox Buddhist milieu; when you came into his house you entered the Buddhist world.

But when I visited Bandjaransari I came into an orthodox Muslim world. My parents were liberal Protestants but in reality I grew up in a multi-cultural environment. Buddhists, Muslims, they were my school friends. The European kids formed a small minority.'

Did you have really intimate friends?
'When I was sixteen I lived in the ninth house my parents had had. I was never longer than one or, at most, two years in any one school, except for the high school on Java. I did not have the opportunity to maintain friendships. I even lived in Rotterdam for a year and a half around my tenth year. That was a European way station. After that, we went back to Java. And always I had to start from scratch.'

Frequent moves, many different cultural settings . . . An important characteristic of your youth seems to be mobility.
'I was forced to understand all kinds of social and religious customs I didn't know at home. Because of that, I have learned to adapt to the most varied surroundings. I learned very early on that people can be totally different from the way you are yourself. But, different customs and cultures also really interested me. There was not only the external necessity, but also an inner need.

Especially this Dul, the house boy, taught me a lot. He had been a wayang player and from him I learned to know

[4]Translator's note: the word *Indo* was used for a person with mixed Indonesian and Dutch blood. *Indo* is also used for people from Indonesia.

14

the meaning, for instance, of the gestures that belonged to that shadow play. But irrespective of the external social and cultural circumstances, you can say that growing up in the Dutch East Indies brought with it something else. Your etheric body is formed very differently than in Holland because on those islands there is a very different elemental environment.

That's why, when in 1929 I met Dr Ita Wegman[5], in no more than five minutes we had a mutual sense of recognition. She too had lived on Java until her eighteenth year, she in the Eastern part, I on Central Java. I think she had also looked for an incarnation in which she could develop a mobile imaginative life.

Besides the characteristic of this mobility, my youth had another characteristic, namely that of inner loneliness. I grew up in a vacuum and lived with questions and feelings that weren't really discussed in my immediate surroundings.'

You mean at home?
'My mother was a very plucky woman. She was a fervent feminist and the first president of the Association for Women's Suffrage in the Dutch East Indies. It was unbearable to her that women came in second place. I can still hear her: the fact that you have to hold out your hand for household money! That you can't go out and earn it yourself!

She was entirely right of course. But in our home her attitude sometimes caused some spasmodic situations. Not that my father did not agree with her, he did, but this continuous battle of my mother's caused tensions that left no room for the inner questions I had. The financial and

[5]Translator's note: Dr. Wegman was a physician and one of Rudolf Steiner's closest co-workers.

political independence of women was always number one. And she also expected of her children that they would exert themselves to realize an independent future for themselves. If sometimes you just sat reading a beautiful book she would soon consider that a waste of time. She had one great fear: to grow old in poverty. Everything she did was to prevent that from happening. As a child I often experienced that as oppressive, you always had to do something useful.'

And your father?
'My father was of great significance for my inner development. He was a reporter and editor in chief of *The Locomotive*, the largest newspaper in the Dutch East Indies. His whole life he fought against the excesses of colonialism. In Medan, he fought the mentality of the gentlemen of the tobacco plantations. One deep impression on me came from his fight against the so-called penal sanctions. The Javanese coolies were pressed into service on Java. They had to mark a piece of paper with a cross, and later it became clear they had signed up to work for ten years on the tobacco plantations. So they were away from their families for ten years. If they fled they were fetched back by the police. My father always said: this is an unlawful form of slavery for which we will have to pay heavily.

In these kinds of things he was always the protestor. There were also Chinese coolies who were recruited via Singapore, but these were paid in Singapore dollars. At the end of the month, the Westerners went to the banks to exchange Dutch money for Singapore dollars. As a consequence, the rate of exchange of those dollars would always rise sharply at the end of the month and at the beginning of the month it declined again. That worked against the common man: as soon as he had money at his disposal its value had gone down. My father fought that practice too; he

16

brought it about that the guilder became generally accepted for the payment of wages.

He had an incredibly strong feeling for justice. I remember how he came home one day and told us about an editor with whom he had great difficulty. As city editor, this man often made blunders which led to emotional reactions among the readers. I said to him: but father, you are the boss, aren't you? If you have such problems with him why don't you fire him? He then said to me: listen carefully, as long as that man annoys me I can't fire him. Because then I do him an injustice. I can only fire him when I am no longer annoyed at him. These words have remained at the foundation of all my *personal* work for the rest of my life.'

Did your father feel inwardly related to a man like Multatuli?[6]
'Not at all. My father was often called a socialist but he wasn't at all. He belonged to the Nieuwe Rotterdamsche Courant (one of the principal independent newspapers in Holland – transl.). When he went back to Holland he returned to work there. That was his atmosphere. Left or right in politics had no interest for him.'

The soul, yellow with black spots

'One night just before my second year – I lived in Medan, Sumatra at the time – I had an acute case of cholera, together with eight other children close by. High fever, tremendous diarrhoea, quick dehydration . . . Seven of

[6]Translator's note: Multatuli is the pen name of the nineteenth century Dutch author Eduard Doutres Dekker who wrote several books about Indonesia and Holland with a strong socially critical tenor. Multatuli means, 'he who had much sorrow.'

those kids died in the course of the next day. Of course, I have sometimes wondered why I was one of the two who were allowed to stay alive.

Because of the dehydration, injuries had occurred in my body. The right side of my body was completely paralysed. That's why I had to learn to walk for a second time when I was four. My earliest memory is that I am lying on a mattress in the garden trying to cut out illustrations from a fashion magazine. My mother comes along carrying my younger sister on her arm and says to me: we are going to feed the chickens. I call out: I want to come too! No, is the answer, I can't carry two children . . . I remember very well how I felt when she walked away with my sister on her arm: powerless. I wanted to walk!

Although the paralysis healed itself gradually, there has always remained a slight disorder in the right arm. Because of it, I had as a child, and also later as an adult, a very bad handwriting. No one ever showed understanding for it. I always got hell for it.

Because of the consequences of the paralysis, I was completely unable to hold my own physically among my contemporaries. When someone pushed me I fell over. I could not participate in sports. Until my twelfth year this inability to participate played an important role. As a consequence, I withdrew strongly into myself; I preferred to be in my own inner world. Because of this orientation to my inner life, because of the relatively strong development of my life of imagination and fantasy, this episode has proven to be of great importance for the rest of my life. But to some extent also because I always had a bit of a feeling of being somewhat weaker than others.'

Is the paralysis completely gone?
'I still have to be very careful, for instance, when I pick up a cup of coffee. If I don't watch out I will easily knock it over.

However, I have learned to adapt to it and almost no one notices it any more. When I write a letter the first five lines will be readable but then the trembling and the scribbles begin. Then I hold my right arm with my left hand to guide it or I wait a little while and continue writing when it feels better again. Therefore, after I had written many of my books I dictated them onto a tape and had them transcribed by a typist. The tape we are using now still has the dictation for the book *Man on the Threshold*. Funny, isn't it?'

You said, "I withdrew into my inner world".
'I brooded a lot, and had many fantasies, and was busy with questions other kids did not have. In my eighth year, for instance, I wanted to know what the human soul looked like. I knew I did not need to try such a question on my parents. They had a religious orientation all right but they did not get into such things.

But one day I saw my opportunity. We were on vacation in the mountains of the Batak area with a catholic family. They had a son of my age. We were hiking one day and this boy and I were walking behind our parents. Because I thought catholic people knew such things I asked him if he knew what the soul looked like. Yellow, with black spots, and those black spots are your sins, was the prompt answer. Would you believe that is the way I always visualized the soul until deep into my thirties: yellow with black spots! That question was a first attempt at getting to know something about things with which no one in my surroundings was concerned.

A fateful prediction

'I was about thirteen years old – we lived in Semarang – when my sister Toni said to me one day that when cleaning a closet she had found two horoscopes, one for her and one for me. A younger brother of my mother was a captain in the merchant marine; he dabbled in astrology and at sea he had a lot of time to make horoscopes. My sister had read those horoscopes and said: Bernard, now I know what is going to happen to us in the future; listen, you will get married but your wife will soon die and then you will marry a second time and that marriage will last a very long time!

I was really horrified at hearing this. This knowledge put a damper on my entire puberty and adolescence. Always when I fell in love I thought, my God, don't let me fall in love because then the girl will die. Once I forgot this knowledge. I was twenty-one, lived already in Holland and met Truus Hinse in Groningen, a cousin of my best friend. I was rather shy – I still am although you might not say so now. I still often procrastinate when I have to call someone because I think that I might disturb them . . .

So, I was very shy, but when I saw this girl it was love at first sight. A very intense relationship grew at that time. She had a quiet, introverted personality, in many respects the opposite of mine. A mature soul. I married her in 1931. But the predicted tragedy did happen, in 1932. Five weeks after the birth of our first child Truus died. I had in the meantime become a physician and had already become deeply involved in anthroposophical work. Suddenly I was alone with a child of a few weeks. We had been engaged for four years and married less than one.

There are events in life that always stay in the present, deep inside, that never soften or wear off. This is one of those. Even now, I feel I miss her deeply, I feel a big loss. I only need to sink into myself for a moment and I experience it again. The pain of the death of that woman has never disappeared. And maybe it is good to say openly that for a long time much of my work in the anthroposophical movement was a flight from this pain.

Sometimes people said with admiration: Bernard, you are doing so much! And it is true, I have done a lot in my life. But the grief over the loss of this relationship was a hidden motive for many years. You know, you have to be very close to people to really be familiar with their inner motives. The surface is just an appearance. The same goes for my shyness.'

You don't make a shy impression.
'People think I am a decisive person and in a certain sense, that is true. But inside, I often feel this shyness, even now that I am eighty-five and have had a life that doesn't exactly make one think of shyness.'

Later, you married again.
'It was a great happiness for me that after the death of my first wife a new intense relationship grew, with Nel Schatborn, Truus' best friend. From that relationship, the second marriage came about that was mentioned in the horoscope. And indeed, that marriage has lasted a long time, until this day, more than fifty-five years. A very happy bond. Six children were born from it. In addition, Nel and I share the same involvement in anthroposophy. This has proven to be very important. It enables us both to direct ourselves with heart and soul to the things that are important to us.

You can imagine that because of this whole story I have often thought about astrology. On the one hand you see that astrology isn't all nonsense. It is an extremely old science, a degenerated echo of old mystery wisdom. But on the other hand, you see how disastrous it can be to have knowledge of things that are to happen in the future. You are inwardly inhibited by them, you lose your spontaneity. Astrology in its present form can be an abomination for people. No, I am definitely not a friend of it.'

21

Too late at the temple

'As a child I often had the same dream. For years it came back again and again. The course of my life has shown that this dream was not just a dream. In a certain sense, it was a picture of one of the central themes of my life. I dreamed I saw a hill with a wooden temple on the top. I stood at the bottom of the hill at the beginning of a path that wound its way up and I thought: I have got to get up there! But always, the dream ended as soon as I began to climb. Never did I reach the top.

This dream strongly dominated me. My mother commissioned a Javanese carpenter to make a big box for my building blocks, incredibly heavy, for those big blocks, you know. It had all kinds of things in it, pillars, arches, blocks. I built a Greek temple of these on the table in my bedroom. When it got dark I turned off all the lights and put a candle on the altar I had made inside the temple. Then I sat on the floor and looked up to the candlelight I could see between the columns and had the feeling: now I am close to that temple. This temple stood on my table for months and months until my mother said it had to go. She thought it was all nonsense.

Many years later – I was in high school in Semarang, Java and was preparing for the final exams – my sister Toni suddenly fell seriously ill with malaria. She had to go to Switzerland for a cure. I went with her and my mother to Europe and was dropped off with a family in The Hague. In April 1924, someone visited this family, a theosophist who said that on his trip to Europe he had stopped off in Basel to see the temple of the anthroposophists. They had built a wooden temple on top of a hill . . .

Then he told us how "the Catholics" had burned the temple down and that there was nothing left of it. When I heard that I thought: my God, then I am too late! I won't see my temple any more! I don't remember whether the man used the word Goetheanum. But during his story the shivers ran over my back, from the top down and from the bottom up. You only get that feeling with tremendous emotions. I thought, oh my God . . .

I also remember the man telling us about the little posts that lined the road up the hill. The tops of these posts were bent. He met someone there with a black hat and a terribly gloomy face who declared that those posts were there to foster humility. Everyone had to laugh when the man was telling this story, but I just sat there trembling.

That was my first encounter with anthroposophy although it was only later that I understood that the man had spoken about the Goetheanum. When I heard the story I was eighteen years and seven months old. That was, therefore, my first "moon node" (ie the return of the moon's position at a person's birth vis-à-vis the sun – JvdM). Looking back, you get the feeling that the meeting with this man, exactly at that moment, had been hidden in my karma.'

So you came too late?
'That same year, Rudolf Steiner was in The Hague at the foundation of the Anthroposophical Society in The Netherlands. I was busy with my final high school exams at that time and therefore did not meet him. Nor did I later, and in 1925 Steiner died. Indeed, I have often had the feeling of having come too late.'

II. The encounter with anthroposophy

In 1924, Bernard Lievegoed begins his medical studies in Groningen. During those first study years, he meets anthroposophy and also a few important anthroposophical friends such as Ita Wegman and Willem Zeylmans van Emmichoven. Rapidly he gets involved in the development of the anthroposophical movement, both in Holland and in Switzerland and Germany. In 1930, he graduates in Amsterdam as a general physician. In the same year, together with Willem Zeylmans, then chairman of the Anthroposophical Society in The Netherlands and author of a number of books, he organizes a large international anthroposophical youth camp. Right after the camp he decides to focus on curative education, the anthroposophical care and nursing of developmentally disturbed children, and he starts 'Zonnehuis' in 1931, the first curative educational institute in Holland. In 1939, Lievegoed gets his MD with the thesis *Maat, ritme, melodie. Grondslagen voor een therapeutisch gebruik van musicale elementen.*[7]

I only saw her hands

'In 1923, when I was eighteen, I went to Europe. Originally I had had the idea to study electrotechnology. My entire room was crisscrossed by wires; there was live current on

[7]Not available in English. Translated, the title might read: Measure, Rhythm, and Melody – Fundamentals for Therapeutical Use of Musical Elements.

24

the door handle and first you had to ring a bell three times before I would turn off the current. Later I thought it had better be chemistry. The same man who had told me about the burned down temple had a son who also studied chemistry and this boy and a few friends then told me about that field of study.

That was on the seafront in Scheveningen, I can still show you the bench where we sat. One of them told me he had a job at Sikkens and another one also had some job already. But I became quieter and quieter and thought: the subject is interesting of course, but do I want to spend my life in a factory? Shortly thereafter, I decided to study medicine. With that, I could still do anything I wanted; I could become a physician or follow a scientific career . . .

I wrote my parents a letter and asked for their permission. By coincidence, my sister came across this letter years later. When I reread it after so many years I really had to laugh about it. Good heavens, I surely made it look beautiful! I wrote it was such a noble profession in which you could help people. But in essence, I chose the subject because I did not want to commit myself yet. I wanted to be free.

I chose Groningen. I did not want to go to Leiden because all my friends from the East Indies were there and I wanted to free myself from them. Groningen was good and far away. There I was busy for quite a few years with research into cancer cells in the body, under the supervision of Professor Deelman, then the great cancer specialist in Holland. I had to look for possible cell mutations in the vicinity of cancer cells.

All my free time I invested in that research, and when I had received my master's degree I told the professor I was quitting. He said: another six months and you can write your thesis about it. I replied: when I have written that thesis it will stand among all those other theses in your book

25

case and no one will ever look at it again. Getting an MD is a one-time event in life and I will get it on a subject I really believe in. I want to do more than only add a grain of sand to the sea of facts that are already known.

I went to Amsterdam and later visited the psychiatrist Professor Carp. He knew I had in the meantime become an anthroposophist and agreed that I would write a thesis about the fundamentals of musical therapy. Carp was a noble man, but also a lonely figure. He was a very reserved person and could come across as contorted. From him I learned psychiatry as a discipline. My MD was for me an intermediate stage; I wanted a scientific title to be able to feel at home in an official way in the world of psychiatry. The title of the thesis was: *Maat, ritme, melodie. Grondslagen voor een therapeutisch gebruik van musicale elementen.*[8] It was republished in 1983.'

Your encounter with anthroposophy . . .
'I sketched the first encounter for you. That happened quite unconsciously. The second one was in the spring of 1926. My parents were returning to Holland and I travelled with my sister to Genoa to pick them up from the boat. After that, we were going with the whole family to Rome to look at art and then have a vacation in Switzerland. When we arrived in Switzerland there was a letter waiting for us from Els Joekes, the mother of a famous Dutch politician; my parents were close friends of the Joekes family. The letter, that was addressed to my mother, read as follows: Dear Marie, when you are back in Holland, you should quickly come to see me because I have found here what we could never find in the Dutch East Indies. I very much want you to get to know it.

[8]See note 7 on page 24

That was anthroposophy. When we were back in Holland, Els Joekes immediately gave me the 'blue book' by Ita Wegman and Rudolf Steiner about anthroposophy and medicine (*Fundamentals of Therapy, An Extension of the Art of Healing through Spiritual Knowledge* – JvdM). I began to read it right away and thought: this is it! During the physiology classes I had always had the feeling that the way things were represented there was only partially right. When I read in this book about the ether body and the astral body I thought: these are concepts I can work with.'

You did not find them strange in any way?
'On the contrary, there was a complete inner agreement. But because it was right before my bachelor's exam, and I was afraid I would never finish my studies if I threw myself into anthroposophy, I put that book away after two chapters. Finish my studies as fast as possible and then be a free man!'

When did the first contacts with anthroposophists come about?
'In 1926, I had attended the first anthroposophical pedagogical conference, in the Pulchri Studio in The Hague. There I met for the first time all those co-workers of Rudolf Steiner, the great pioneers of the anthroposophical movement who have played such an important role in the rest of my life. For instance, Willem Zeylmans van Emmichoven was there, the chairman of the Anthroposophical Society in The Netherlands. Also, Herbert Hahn, Walter Johannes Stein and Eugen Kolisko, Caroline von Heydebrand, etcetera. I still remember Kolisko coming up to the rostrum and saying with his easy-going Austrian accent: 'Brille für das Auge ist gleich Plattfusseinlage für den Plattfuss.' (Eyeglasses for the eyes are as arch supports for flat feet – transl.)
Those people were really something. Walter Johannes

Stein, for instance, he thundered his lecture into the hall. Later, I got to know Herbert Hahn very well because he came to live with us in Zeist. He could tell stories about Rudolf Steiner in such a way that you felt you had known him yourself. But I also let others talk to me about Rudolf Steiner. Steiner through the eyes of Stein, Steiner through the eyes of Kolisko, Steiner through the eyes of Zeylmans.

You had the feeling that Steiner, who had died just over a year before, continued to live in the aura of those people. You heard his voice right through the voices of the people. In a way, you could hear him again and again, from different sides. Steiner through Stein, Steiner through Zeylmans . . . Sometimes I told myself: don't fool yourself, you never knew Steiner yourself!

I remember Herbert Hahn saying once in 1932; you know what is the tragedy of our generation? We are becoming more and more like ourselves. We are falling back into our personal karma. When Rudolf Steiner was still alive we were lifted up far out of ourselves. We were able to do infinitely more because of his presence.'

Did you soon go to Dornach, the place where Rudolf Steiner had worked the last years of his life and where the second Goetheanum was built?

'In 1928 or '29, with my parents. When we were there a performance took place of *The Guardian of the Threshold*, Rudolf Steiner's third mystery drama. In the intermission, I took a little walk with my father in the field behind the Goetheanum where nothing had been built yet at the time, further up the hill, until we were high enough to look down on the roof. I asked my father: well, what do you think of it? With a perfect sentence, as always, he replied: I believe I can observe with clarity that from now on we will be unable to avoid this. He also became an anthroposophist, in his own way. Actually, he was more of a poet than a reporter.'

28

But didn't you realize then: this is the place where the temple stood which I have not been able to see any more?
'Of course I did. Only, you shouldn't forget that in 1928 the second Goetheanum was just finished, the concrete building that is still standing there now. In part, the scaffolding was still standing, everything was bare, the stairs were not covered, iron stuck out everywhere . . . The building did make a deep impression on me, but it was not my temple. And it never became my temple even though I have been there so many times. No, I would have experienced the first Goetheanum very differently.

In the summer of 1929, I went again and that time I also visited the clinic in Arlesheim, a few miles from the Goetheanum. That clinic had been founded by Ita Wegman in cooperation with Rudolf Steiner. I came out of the blazing sun into a completely dark space and stood somewhere waiting when suddenly a door opened and someone came in my direction. It proved to be Doctor Margarete Bockholt with whom I would later often cooperate. Almost half a century later, she wrote a book, together with her husband Erich Kirchner, about Rudolf Steiner and Ita Wegman. (*Rudolf Steiner's Mission and Ita Wegman* – JvdM)

When a little later I was sitting at the dinner table there I said to myself: finally, I am home! I said that literally: I am home! Wherever I went I always felt like a guest, also in my youth. That day, I also had my first conversation with Ita Wegman.'

What impression did she make?
'I had seen her once before in The Hague, at a meeting of physicians after the opening of the Rudolf Steiner Clinic. That meeting ended at six in the evening and then it was announced that Ita Wegman would arrive later in the evening. I had heard a lot about her already and of course

knew she had written that book about medicine together with Rudolf Steiner. I wanted to meet her and therefore I hung around.

Nine o'clock passed, ten o'clock . . . and at a quarter past ten the door of the dining room suddenly opened and there she came in. A tall lady with a big fox around her shoulders. She sat down in a chair and looked around pulling the fox around her again and again. Then she put her hands in her lap and I thought: such remarkable hands. I kept looking at those hands. In the last train back to Amsterdam, I thought: I don't even know what her face looks like, I have only seen her hands.'

What was it about those hands?
'They were very expressive hands, slender hands with long fingers. Something very unusual expressed itself in those hands. Besides being a physician, Ita Wegman was also a masseuse.'

How can you describe her personality?
'She had a simple, open personality with a great interest in everyone. She always tried to cheer people up, to encourage them. She had an enormous respect for the choices people made for themselves. But she was also realistic. When one day I had a conversation with her about the possibility of starting a curative educational institute in Holland she said just before leaving: one more thing, can you handle disappointments? I asked her what she meant. In curative education, she said, it can happen to you that you have worked with a child for five years and that it has made tremendous progress. But then the parents take the child away because a little hat got lost somewhere in the garden. Could you handle that?

Of course, I said. Now, now, she said, all right, just think about it a bit. Ita Wegman was a most spiritual woman but also a practical one. And she was right: you can only work in anthroposophy if you can get over disappointments. After this visit to the clinic in Arlesheim, I joined the Anthroposophical Society. That was quite a step. In those days it was still just like becoming a catholic.'

Inner preparation

'Actually, it can be said that my life only started the moment I came in contact with anthroposophy. Everything before that was a dream. I was twenty-four when I had my medical diploma in my pocket and, surprised, I wondered: what have you really done for it, everything went automatically, didn't it? I had no trouble learning so it really was no merit.

In 1930, suddenly the moment of self-knowledge arrived. Willem Zeylmans had asked me to assume the organization of a large international anthroposophical youth camp, the camp *De Stakenberg*. We younger people had the feeling there were dark times coming. The National Socialists in Germany were becoming stronger all the time and in the Anthroposophical Society there were big problems. Zeylmans had the feeling in 1930 that it was still possible. He wanted to organize a large anthroposophical meeting as a positive gesture against all the awful things that were threatening the world.

Looking back, we realize he was right. When the Nazis had come to power in Germany in 1933, it soon became clear such things would no longer be possible. At a very early stage, Willem Zeylmans, Walter Johannes Stein and Eugen Kolisko had a sharp insight into the fate that was awaiting Europe. One more time a meeting in which young people of every possible nationality would be together: that was the motive for organizing the camp.

31

Alright, so I became the organizer. During the preparations, a kind old lady came to me in the grounds of the camp and said: Gee, Mr. Lievegoed, I hear you studied medicine. Do you have your bachelor's degree yet? I replied: yes madam, I even have my master's. Really now, said the lady, you don't say, you are still so young . . . And I again: Yes madam, but that gets a little better every day. And feeling angry I walked away.

But inside I thought, the woman is right. I looked in the mirror and realized I looked like someone of seventeen. My father also always looked much younger than he was. That was something hereditary and, therefore, again no merit. I thought: can I, with this appearance, start a medical practice as a physician? The patients will burst out laughing when they see me sitting in my office! That was the first point: it was suddenly clear to me that I might have this diploma in my pocket but that did not mean I was a physician by a long shot.

The second point was that I thought: I want to link my professional work with anthroposophy. At that time, I had contacts going with the cancer institute in Amsterdam and I had arranged with the people there that I would continue my scientific work. During camp *De Stakenberg*, however, I inwardly resolved to give this up. I had the feeling that this kind of scientific research and anthroposophy were too far removed from each other. I then determined to prepare myself inwardly for the work in curative education. A little more than a year later, I founded in Bosch en Duin the first curative educational institute in Holland, "Zonnehuis". Later, that institute moved to Veldheim in Zeist, one of the houses where it still is now.

My choice for anthroposophy and for a professional life in the anthroposophical movement immediately had big consequences. Very soon, I was asked by Willem Zeylmans to join the Council of the Anthroposophical Society. That way, I developed a close relationship with Zeylmans. I also started a very intensive study of anthroposophy.'

Were there any specific themes that occupied you in your studies?
'The main points were the qualities of the seven planets and the concept of development, in all its facets. Again and again, I came back to the question: What is development? What are the laws of development, how do they work in bio-dynamic farming, in the growing child, in organizations, in history? The basic book for me was, therefore, *Occult Science, An Outline* in which Rudolf Steiner sketches the big picture of the development of mankind. And also the lecture cycle *True and False Paths in Spiritual Investigation* of 1924 in which he further elaborated the theme.'

What importance did Zeylmans have for you?
'My real teacher was Rudolf Steiner. But Willem Zeylmans and Ita Wegman also played a big part as teachers, especially in a practical way. With them I could speak in a very concrete manner about all sorts of factual matters. Zeylmans was an example for me in the way he took hold of things. He had a deep esoteric insight into anthroposophy and the development of the anthroposophical movement. He never spoke about side issues; he always called attention to essential things. Willem Zeylmans had a very intense inner life.

The first time I met Zeylmans was in 1926 at the first pedagogical conference in The Hague. I was sitting in the back of the large hall of Pulchri when Zeylmans came in with some other participants. In a crowd, his whole head would stick out above the surrounding people. He was just a very tall man; to talk with someone he almost always had to bend his head and talk down to them 'from above'. Some people did not understand that and found him proud and detached.

33

Zeylmans looked a lot older than he really was. He made the impression on me of a truly ancient soul. He must have been among the hierophants in the old mysteries many, many times. I experienced myself as his pupil. Later I learned that the relationship of the teacher to the pupil in the old mysteries was not one-sided: the teacher needs the pupil just as much as the pupil the teacher.

We were very different people and were conscious of that. He had a strong imaginative life and was able to put deep truths into words. He was also a bit of a loner, he was at his most creative when he was alone with himself. I was more a will person, more oriented towards doing things and flourished especially in cooperation with other people. All by myself I am not worth much. But because we were conscious of those differences we could work together very well. That became clear, for instance, in the camp *De Stakenberg* which was his idea and for which one could say that he provided the content. I was the organizer and executed the idea. He would sometimes say: I am too lazy for such things.

Willem Zeylmans remained my teacher to the last moment of his life. Within the anthroposophical movement, he was an original thinker. His whole stature was saturnine, in his face the skeleton dominated. His forehead revealed the encompassing thinker. He was a spiritual eagle that hovered far above the earth. With the people to whom he gave his confidence, he had a relationship of deeply hidden warmth and absolute loyalty. In such a relationship, time became something infinite: when you had had a profound conversation with him it could suffice for a couple of years.

Vis-à-vis people, he took a position that for him, as psychiatrist and psychotherapist, was a matter of course: an absolute respect for the inner world of every other person, also when, by accepted standards, the person was wrong.

He practised this attitude also in his judgments of people and situations. I learned from him that the same facts can be observed from different points of view and that more than one standpoint is possible. Without this attitude to life, he would not have lived through the storms in the anthroposophical movement in the thirties.

Zeylmans was an independent spiritual investigator, his judgments were based on inner experiences. These experiences arose in him as pictures when awakening from sleep. That happened, as he said, after he had for a long time posed a question to the spiritual world. He hardly ever spoke about these pictures but they gave him strength and certainty. More than once he said to me: "What we have talked about is for me a certainty. But you must not believe me on my authority. Take it as a working hypothesis and see whether or not it bears fruit for you."

Central in his life was his inner 'birth' when attending the Christmas meeting of 1923. He always spoke about the importance of the Christmas meeting of 1923, the so-called *Weihnachtstagung* during which the anthroposophical movement underwent an important renewal. Again and again, he emphasized how that Christmas meeting had been an exceptional, unique moment in the development of anthroposophy. For people who have never made a study of Rudolf Steiner's life and the development of anthroposophy it has always been hard to understand why just this meeting was so crucial, not only for anthroposophists but for all mankind. Something like that sounds strange and exaggerated, and yet it is true.'

How did Zeylmans describe the importance of that meeting?
'At the core, he always said: in 1923, the new mysteries were established, mysteries that fit the consciousness of modern man. The new organization of the Anthroposophical Society was meant for the realization of these new

mysteries just like the establishment of the School for Spiritual Science that was founded during the same meeting. Willem Zeylmans also always spoke about the Foundation Stone, the verse pronounced by Rudolf Steiner during that meeting. Both of us have written about the Foundation Stone, Zeylmans in 1956 and I in 1987.

The fact that Zeylmans put so much emphasis on that Christmas meeting was not a common thing in the thirties, not even in anthroposophical circles. In Dornach, the center of the international movement, people really paid but little attention to that meeting. When you mentioned the Christmas meeting people would say: which Christmas meeting, wasn't there a Christmas meeting every year? Zeylmans really went against the tide with that theme. In the meantime, that fortunately has changed; now everyone in the anthroposophical movement is convinced that something truly essential happened in those last days of 1923 and the first days of 1924.

Really tragic was the fact that Zeylmans' constant calling attention to the Christmas meeting was considered by others, including anthroposophists, as political ambition. People thought Zeylmans was looking for a mission to make himself important in the international society. They said about him that in reality he was power hungry. But that was so far from the truth! He had personally been present at the Christmas meeting of 1923; the events there had become the center of his life.'

So the relationships you found in the anthroposophical movement were not simple.
'After the death of Rudolf Steiner in 1925, big problems arose in the anthroposophical movement. Enormous differences became visible. Of course, these were already there when Steiner was still alive but they remained

36

underground. Steiner had the capability of enabling people of totally different karmic backgrounds to work together.

In my latest book, *Mensheidsperspectiven*[9], I have tried to indicate these karmic backgrounds. Some people carried with them from prior lives more of a Greek disposition and lived out of the Greek mysteries; others were inwardly more oriented to the Egyptian mysteries, or the Celtic ones. You have to imagine that around Rudolf Steiner a group of co-workers had come together with a variety of karmic backgrounds. In many cases, co-workers had fought each other in a previous life and now they had to work together. Have no illusions about the emotions this can call forth. Karma works!

Aristotelians and Platonists had to work together. How many times have those two streams opposed each other in history! Life and death struggles! From 1923 on, Rudolf Steiner's actual assignment to his co-workers was: In the framework of the newly-founded society, exercise tolerance. Work with each other. Perhaps that sounds trivial but more is involved than, for instance, merely accommodating the personal limitations and incapacities of others. One person has a different mystery background than another and that is why there are differences that transcend the personal. The difficulty is, of course, that such suprapersonal differences often present themselves as personal ones. That is why it often seems as though a struggle is taking place that is bound to the persons involved. And in a certain sense of course, that is true too. But the essential point in social intercourse is to develop the power of imagination through which you can really understand and accept the karmic backgrounds of others, although these can be very different from your own.

When I came into contact with anthroposophy and

[9]See note 3 on page 7.

anthroposophists of course I knew nothing about that. I was still completely innocent and, in addition, I had the ability to get along with practically everyone. That is what got me into trouble sometimes.'

What trouble?
'Gradually I began to notice that you were judged and used by others against the background of the conflicts. There were camps, and everyone tested everyone with the hidden question to which camp they belonged. For instance, you had the camp around Albert Steffen, the Swiss poet who succeeded Rudolf Steiner after his death as chairman of the international society. And you had the camp around Marie Steiner, Rudolf Steiner's wife. But other persons also played an important role, such as Ita Wegman and Willem Zeylmans.

For myself, I soon had the feeling I had no karmic connection with that struggle. It is not my destiny, as it was for my friend Willem Zeylmans, to wage this battle. Perhaps if I had become involved with anthroposophy a few years earlier it would have been very different. I had the feeling my task was in a completely different direction. I have always been able to maintain friendships in all camps.'

What were the concrete points of contention?
'There were lots of them! But an important moment came in 1932, when Albert Steffen, then chairman of the international society, said in a meeting: 'I can only recognize anthroposophists who follow the "correct method"' and 'in my section I can only work with people who are able to write a treatise on the level of the esthetic letters of Schiller.' When I heard him say that I thought: my good man, can you do that yourself?

Albert Steffen certainly did not mean any harm. But that was the moment when the struggle for the correct method began. One person regarded another as dangerous because he did not follow the correct method. Only, anthroposophy is no method. Anthroposophy wants to awaken in individual people the potential to act out of their own spiritual insight and freedom. If you don't do that, and you work exclusively out of the books, then indeed you follow a method.

In those times, I learned much from Ita Wegman. I sat in the hall during the meetings in Dornach and while really awful things were being said, also about her as a person, she just stayed in her seat and kept silent. Afterwards, we asked her why she had not said anything. Then she answered: Dr. Steiner taught me you can't fight demons; you can only starve them to death by not feeding them. She had a very strong, sovereign personality. The miserable part of the situation was that the persons who had been asked into the Vorstand by Rudolf Steiner in 1923, such as Albert Steffen, Ita Wegman, and Marie Steiner-Von Sivers, became more and more alienated from each other.

Originally, Zeylmans and Steffen had been great friends. They once made a three day walking trip through England together. Ita Wegman too, had a friendship with Steffen. When there was a festivity for the patients in Ita Wegman's clinic Albert Steffen would come with his magic show. That was his hobby. In the later conditions, that was unthinkable. As younger people, we had the feeling that a dark cloud cast a shadow not only over the society but also over Europe. In the society, there were these disastrous conflicts, in Europe the emergence of Nazism.

In my personal life there was also the loss of my first wife in those years. One evening, I was in The Hague where Herbert Hahn spoke in the Waldorf school about Goethe on the occasion of the bicentennial of his death. Afterwards, we sat together talking in Pieter de Haan's house (an active

39

anthroposophist who among other things published trans-
lations of books by Rudolf Steiner – JvdM) when there was
this telephone call from the nurse. Could I quickly come to
Zeist because my wife had a high fever. I went home and
thought, oh my God, that horoscope . . . Right after all . . .
Fate is carried out . . . All those years, I had not thought
about it any more. With the anthroposophical physician
Galjart from The Hague, I stood at that sickbed and there
was nothing we could do.

I lived in two worlds at that time. In my private life there
was the inner trial, in the world around me there were the
fights. In those difficult years I began to understand that life
itself is the most important schooling.'

What was it that life taught you?
'That is hard to put into words. Rudolf Steiner once said
that wisdom is crystallized suffering. The fact that in your
life you can give something to others, no matter how little it
sometimes seems to be, is directly related to the sorrows
and grief you carry around with you. Everything good
comes from sacrifice.'

Seemingly defeated

'Looking back to the thirties you have to wonder how it was
possible that the anthroposophical movement did not
understand what was really crucial. Rudolf Steiner had
often spoken about the beginning of the thirties and said
that in those years an important event would take place in
the spiritual world, namely the appearance of Christ in the
etheric world. How often did he not say: it is of the greatest
importance that people do not "sleep through" this event,
and he considered it the task of the anthroposophical
movement to wake people up to this fact.'

What is meant by the appearance of Christ in the etheric world?

'Rudolf Steiner often stated that Christ has a central role in the development of mankind. He described Christ as a divine being who joined himself for a period of three years with the human individuality we know as Jesus of Nazareth. The purpose of this was the sacrifice on the cross of Golgotha. The death of Christ was a sacrifice for humanity; because of his *earthly* death, and the resurrection that followed it, every man could, from that time on, in his own inner being, have access to his own I. In a certain sense you can say Christ has granted all people their I and, in so doing, their freedom, their spiritual autonomy. That is the deeper significance of the mystery of Golgotha.

After this mystery of Golgotha, ie after the Ascension, Christ remains active in the spiritual world. Rudolf Steiner describes how in this spiritual world, in the region that borders directly on the reality of the sense world, namely the etheric region, a new death and a new resurrection of Christ will take place in the twentieth century. Through that resurrection of Christ in the etheric world more and more people will have an experience like the apostle Paul had before the gates of Damascus. With a natural clair-voyance they will *see* the figure of Christ. And this seeing of Christ will generate an inner certainty, an invincible power with which the negative counterforces can be faced. Rudolf Steiner said sometimes it is the task of anthroposophy to awaken people to this experience, to make it clear that it is a concrete spiritual experience.

As the specific year for the appearance of Christ in the etheric he mentioned the year 1933. It is the same year that Hitler came to power in Germany. Nazism, what else was it than an attempt by the opposing powers to distract mankind from experiencing the appearance of Christ in the etheric? By calling up wild emotions, feelings of hate, the

41

souls of men were darkened and they could not observe anything of what happened in the etheric world. Hitler was a medium of demonic beings who go all out to bring about deep inner unrest in people. All the time he worked from a sort of trance condition.'

Was there, in your opinion, a connection between the rise of Nazism and the conflicts in the Society?
'In the Anthroposophical Society the etheric Christ has been talked about. For the demons, therefore, the Society was the greatest enemy. That was where there were people who knew about it. Only, those people might have known about it but they didn't always carry it in their hearts. You must not forget that anthroposophy was understood by many people as something quite intellectual. There were anthroposophists who knew an incredible amount about all the things Rudolf Steiner had said. But Ita Wegman, for instance, was not intellectually oriented at all. She was a highly intuitive personality who did not go the way of gathering knowledge. Many did not understand that. The inability to understand each other, that was the core of the problem.

Rudolf Steiner must have foreseen that. When he was on his deathbed and said to Ita Wegman: all of you must take into account that I will die, and Ita Wegman desperately asked: and what is to become of us? he replied: then karma will work. He meant: then you will all fall back into your own karma. And that is what happened. The forces of integration in the Society were still too weak.'

What was the deeper cause of his premature death?
'In its most profound aspects, Rudolf Steiner's dying is a mystery. Why did he go just at that moment? I don't know. An important event was, of course, the destruction of the first Goetheanum that was lost through fire on New Year's

Eve in 1922. Steiner reputedly said he had been greatly weakened after the fire. Don't forget you build such a building with the forces of your etheric body. Such a great building, that contains something of yourself. Because of the fire he was weakened. His metabolism became worse and worse, his kidneys virtually stopped working and in the end he could not take in food any more.'

Did you often talk with Ita Wegman and Willem Zeylmans about those conflicts?
'There were times when that was all we did talk about. In 1929 when I became a member of the Society I heard about them already. As younger people we worked constantly with the question how we, as a group that had no history in those conflicts, could overcome the conflicts and build a society that was not burdened by them? That was one of our impulses for the organization of camp *De Stakenberg* in 1930 in which indeed all kinds of streams were present among the young people that attended.

That camp was a last effort to put a large anthroposophical manifestation into the world, to bring anthroposophy in a convincing way. A large, powerful, Christian movement. It succeeded too. The young people felt very strongly the threat of National Socialism while the older people in the Society hardly noticed it. I remember I was in Stuttgart for three days in 1934 with Willem Zeylmans and Pieter de Haan to talk with German friends about the problems in the Society. One of those nights was the so-called Roehm night. Roehm was the leader of the SA and more beloved by the people than Hitler who was already in power at that time.

That night, Hitler went to Roehm's headquarters and had him arrested; Later Roehm was executed by the SS. That night, tanks and soldiers went through the streets of Stuttgart, sirens wailed; a curfew was announced over the radio. The all clear signal wasn't given until four in the morning when it was over and we could go back to our hotel. Hitler was afraid of an insurrection of the SA and therefore he had ordered the SS to surround their camps. That Roehm night, terrible, totally demonic.

You lived in those times in an enormous spiritual tension. Will the demons break through or won't they? We experienced those events as a direct assault on the anthroposophical impulse. Looking back you have to say: those who should have been ready in 1933 had been eliminated by the demons.'

You chose to go your own way.

'Exactly. The initiative for camp *De Stakenberg* was attacked by lots of anthroposophists from the moment it was announced. That made us ready to fight. We thought the fact we were being attacked proved we were doing something important; they weren't going to get us down.

For a month, one hundred and twenty students built the camp that took place in the summer of 1930 in the vicinity of Harderwijk: building kitchens, no end of things to organize, setting up tents we had rented from the army, and a large circus tent for twelve hundred people. When we started we were expecting four hundred participants but in the shortest time, there were six hundred applications. In the end the six hundred became one thousand and at that point we said that was the limit.

But on the first day, it turned out twelve hundred people had come from twenty-seven different countries! There was a group of seventeen Romanian students who had come by bicycle across Europe to the camp. From Germany, they came in all sorts of different ways. There were Englishmen, Norwegians, Americans, New Zealanders, you name it. Also all the pioneers were there, Walter Johannes Stein, Eugen Kolisko, Elisabeth Vreede.'

In the anthroposophical movement, the camp caused dissent.
'Many anthroposophists thought it was a superficial undertaking. That was not the way to do anthroposophy. Just imagine, five hundred people doing eurythmy on a moor, in the *open air*! People speaking about anthroposophy in a *circus tent*! It was all proof of our lack of respect for the holy anthroposophy. But there were impressive lectures by Zeylmans, by Walter Johannes Stein. Every important anthroposophical theme was discussed. And there were courses about the natural sciences, medicine, agriculture, etc.

In 1935, the fateful thing happened: Willem Zeylmans, Ita Wegman and many others were expelled against their will as members of the General Anthroposophical Society. In those years – Zeylmans was then about thirty-five – he had a heart attack in the train going home from Dornach and we all thought that was the end of him. About that heart attack he later said himself: the moment I was expelled from the Society I was mortally wounded; it made it impossible to carry out my task. At that time, I experienced Willem Zeylmans as an eagle with clipped wings. He suffered under this tragedy. He would say: what Rudolf Steiner meant with the Christmas meeting of 1923 is now going to be delayed for decades.

What remained? In late 1990, early 1991 we had the Gulf Crisis. In the thirties there was a similar atmosphere, only then right at our front door. From day to day you read in the papers: what has Hitler dreamt up now again? When the war finally broke out in 1939, in a certain sense, that even brought some relief. At that moment, you finally knew what to expect. The looming threat in the thirties was unbearably heavy. And the Anthroposophical Society had lost its right of speaking. If you can't solve your own problems you have no right to offer a solution to the world.

45

In this period, I withdrew strongly into curative education. There we had obvious things to do: helping specific children who were being threatened in their physical, psychic, and spiritual development. We also organized two more camps for young Dutch people, one in 1936 and one in 1938.'

Did you feel defeated?
'We were pushed back into a smaller space but inwardly we were unbeaten. The world was hard to reach. In Germany you couldn't work. And in Dornach, the anthroposophical movement had fallen apart into two camps, one around Albert Steffen and one around Marie Steiner. In Stuttgart, the second important center of the anthroposophical movement, the very first teachers, such as Walter Johannes Stein and Eugen Kolisko, had been forced to leave. Things had lost their lustre. One by one, these teachers went through an enormous inner tragedy: Kolisko died prematurely in 1939, Walter Johannes Stein, part Jew, survived the war but inwardly withered away more and more.'

Walter Johannes Stein fled Germany . . .
'Yes, to England. Life in Germany was too dangerous for him. In addition, he no longer felt at home in Stuttgart and Dornach. Then Herbert Hahn also fled, to Holland, and Ernst Lehrs, and Maria Roeschl, the leader of the Youth Section of the School for Spiritual Science. Everything fell apart.'

How was the situation then in the Dutch Society?
'The international split also had its repercussions in the Dutch situation. There was a minority here that wanted to follow Dornach's lead and a majority that stood behind Willem Zeylmans. The big and terrible meetings in Dornach were repeated here in Holland on a smaller scale.

Only in 1960 did this situation get evened out. As Chairman of the Dutch Society, Willem Zeylmans was continually dedicated to trying to undo the split. In the end, he did succeed. Fifteen years after the war, the reunion took place. For Zeylmans, that had great significance. He wanted to see this conflict resolved for the later generations. But the wound that was caused never completely healed.'

III. The years of building

In 1948, Lievegoed publishes the book *Phases of Childhood*. He gets involved with the establishment of industries in Holland which results in 1954 in the founding of the NPI, an institute for organizational development. In the same year, he becomes Professor of Social Pedagogy at the Netherlands' School of Economics (later Erasmus University) in Rotterdam. In 1961, he succeeds his friend Willem Zeylmans van Emmichoven as Chairman of the Anthroposophical Society in The Netherlands. In 1963, he becomes Dean of the Department of Corporate Science at the School of Technology in Twente and has to create a whole faculty from scratch. In 1971 follows the establishment of the *Vrije Hogeschool* in Driebergen of which he is president until 1982. During these years, he publishes books about organizational development, curative education, developments to be expected in the world at the end of this century, inner development, and mystery streams. In 1983, he receives from the Royal Netherlands Publishers Association the Golden Quill as proof of appreciation for the significance of his published works for Dutch culture.

With a cart through the snow

'Then came in spring of 1939 the preliminary mobilization and I had to report for military service. I was assigned the organization of the psychiatric service for the field army. That was not because I was so unusual but because of my

48

age I happened to have the rank of captain while all the other psychiatrists were lieutenants. I was the head of twenty-four psychiatrists and was based in Utrecht. I had one person above me, a major who, by the way, was a friend of Zeylmans. His name was Jaap Sauvage Nolting and he was an aesthete who loved nothing more than to lie in the sun reading a book. He composed operas for children. I didn't like having someone above me so I said to Sauvage Nolting: Jaap, you sit behind your desk and sign the papers I give you and furthermore you are totally free, you don't need to do a thing. Well, that was a smooth cooperation.

During the mobilization, people were called up who had not seen the inside of any barracks for twenty years and in the meantime had gone schizophrenic. Such people got into the biggest psychological problems. Our task was then to help them, which often meant declaring them unfit for duty. We also had to deal with all cases of stress and mental breakdown. I liked the work because it was something productive to do. That lasted until the German invasion. In the meantime, I also continued to be the leader of *Zonnehuis*, the curative educational institute I had founded in 1931. In November 1939 it had to be evacuated because the main building, *Veldheim*, was to be turned into the headquarters of the field army. General Van Voorst tot Voorst, Chief of Staff of the Dutch army, took over my office.

We ended up in an old sanatorium in Scheveningen, but that did not last long because the army headquarters were, of course, vacated after the invasion and the buildings became available again. So we went back, but in the middle of the war we had to leave again because the Germans had decided to place their navy headquarters in Zeist. There they would be outside the reach of the English guns. Veldheim then became more or less a kind of bordello for a while. We were assigned to the *Witte Hull*, another building in Zeist.

During the "hunger winter" (the winter of 1944-1945 – transl.) we were in the *Witte Hull*. There we had the possibility of taking in many people who had gone into hiding. There were also a couple of Jewish children we were not allowed to have of course. We put them in the garden house of the *Witte Hull*. Later that was not possible any more and we had to look elsewhere to hide them.

The *Witte Hull* was completely surrounded by Waffen-SS troops that had their camp there. With my motorcycle I always had to go right by their sentries to get onto the property. Even when the SS was there we had quite a few people hiding with us. They were safe, exactly because the SS was there. Our fugitives were, in a sense, protected by the SS.

Towards the end of the war, the Germans took away a few of our older boys. They had to dig trenches near Arnhem under fire from the English who were trying to take the bridge over the Rhine there. One of those boys, a mentally retarded man, had no idea of what was going on and kept standing when the English started their fire. He was killed by a bullet. But let me stop with this. So many things happened then . . .'

How did you get food during the hunger winter?
'That was an enormous problem. It so happened that the leader of our bio-dynamic group in Dornach, Heinze, became commander of the German occupying forces in Harlingen. I knew him well because before the war he often came to Loverendale, the first bio-dynamic farm in Holland. Heinze sent us bags of potatoes by ship to Utrecht where we could pick them up. Now and then, he also visited us and then he brought us bread from the officers' mess.

50

With a cart through the snow, fetching the potatoes in Utrecht, miles and miles, hoping the Germans wouldn't catch you, the cold sweat in your shoes . . . I know what it means to be a fugitive, to have no food. You know what it is with war? You get to live totally in the outside world. You live from one day to the next, from one situation to the next. For me at least, I did not lead an inner life, my inner biography in a certain way seemed to have stopped. I was completely oriented to the outer life.

During the war, on top of everything else, we had a scarlet fever epidemic. Fortunately, all the children pulled through, but the consequence was that I got it myself almost a year later. I was very ill, had all kinds of complications such as erysipelas and kidney problems, fever above 106 degrees. But I lay in bed singing, felt great and thought that everyone was worrying about me without reason. Everyone was afraid I would die. But I experienced all sorts of things on that sickbed. One of those things has remained very important to me for the rest of my life.

At the crisis point of the illness I had certain visions. I witnessed what was happening in Russia. And I kept hearing a voice that said: battle of Uman, battle of Uman . . . What I experienced was the retreat of the German troops across an endless plain, troops that went through the landscape in irregular groups without formation. Then appeared a peasant's cart pulled by a horse in which there was a young German soldier, dying. I saw at that moment what the soldier was experiencing: from the distance a figure approached him who waded through the landscape the way you wade through water. A great figure of light. When this figure had come very close the boy died. I experienced this picture so strongly that it stayed with me the whole time and I have often thought: you did not experience that for nothing. In my feeling I have often connected the picture of the dying soldier with the well-

51

known words *In Christo morimur* . . . In Christ we die . . .
Since then, it may really be said, I know what happens
when we die. You must remember that I was also standing
at the edge.'

Because of the war, you said your inner biography had been
stopped. Did the liberation bring the necessary quiet for a more
inward life?
'On the contrary, after the liberation came a busy time.
Zonnehuis had to move back to Veldheim, sixty children
and thirty co-workers emerged from the war unharmed.
And within seven years Zonnehuis grew from sixty children
to about two hundred and thirty. That caused an enormous
amount of problems. In 1947, we added the house *Stenia* so
now Zonnehuis consisted of two houses, one for socially
handicapped children and one for physically handicapped
children. It was a tremendously busy period, nevertheless I
then lived strongly in my inner biography. At that time I
experienced a crisis.

It started when one of our children, Diederik, shortly
after the liberation, fell ill with diptheria and died of it. He
was a little over five years old. Lost. For me that was a
second blow in my personal life. First my first wife, now
this child. I was desperate. Outwardly, everything seemed
to go well: Zonnehuis was growing, we had organized an
anthroposophical summer camp in Blaricum, but inwardly
I wondered what the purpose of my life was. The people
around me told me I had important work to do for the
handicapped children in Zonnehuis. Of course, that was
true, I could not say anything against that. But at night, I
lay awake and kept asking myself the question why twice in
my life I had to lose someone in my immediate family circle.
And what is my actual task in this life? I had the feeling I
had not yet found my destination.

In that situation I received a question from Wim Schukking, then Secretary of the Association for Industry and Commerce, who was looking for people who could say something sensible at the annual meeting of the Association about the industrialization of Holland after the war. There would be someone to talk about financing that industrialization and someone else to deal with the question whether there were enough trained people in Holland, quantitatively, to staff those industries. I was asked to speak about the question of what would have to change in education to make such industrialization possible in a qualitative way.

I got to know Wim Schukking in the war. He lived in a block of houses on a quay in the south of Amsterdam. On Sunday evenings, Hans Heinz, the judge, organized lectures for people in that block. That was during curfew hours so after eight pm you could not walk in the street. Therefore, people climbed out of their attic windows and walked over the flat roof to the house of Hans Heinz. I once gave a talk there about Waldorf education before a group of some twenty people.

Thus, Schukking asked me to speak at this annual meeting about education. I said to him: but Wim, you know my weird ideas about education, don't you? Yes, yes, he said, that is no problem at all, people are eager to hear them. He was right, the lecture was a tremendous success. Then there came lots of questions from local branches of the Association for Industry and Commerce, also from the one in Hengelo. After the lecture, Willem Stork, Social Director of Stork (a manufacturer of industrial machinery – transl.) approached me asking if I was willing to talk with him about certain problems he was having in his company. But I had never been in a large machinery factory!

Well, that was the way I rolled into the business world. It appeared I knew at least something about it. Because of

Zonnehuis and especially because we had gone through a period of rapid growth I knew the organizational problems of growing institutions. One of the mistakes they made at Stork at that time was that they trained many more young people than they could ever place. After that, I went from one company to the next and had to deal everywhere with social problems and questions of training. Everything in Holland was expanding, existing companies had to be reorganized, everything was in development, family businesses with their characteristic pioneer style had to be taken a step forward, you name it.

Early in the fifties, I was asked to take the chair for Social Psychology at the School of Economics in Rotterdam. I turned it down. A year later, they asked me again and then I accepted on condition I could call it Social Ecology. They thought that was crazy, Social Ecology at a school of economics. They proposed Social Pedagogy. And that is what the course was then called.

I did not want to teach from books but from experience, and for that I needed an institute that did factual and practical work in business. In 1954, the *Nederlands Pedagogisch Instituut voor het Bedrijfsleven* was founded and connected with the chair at the School of Economics. This institute would later change its name to NPI – Institute for Organizational Development. I was a co-worker there until 1971.

I wanted to have enough start-up capital to fund five co-workers for a period of two years. A few large companies gave us the money: Shell, Philips, AKZO and Unilever. From De Nederlanden we got the office furniture. Always it was the personnel and training people from the companies who supported us.'

What did the NPI have to do with anthroposophy?
'If you ask me what I really wanted with the NPI my answer

54

is this: From my experiences in the thirties and forties I had drawn the conclusion that anthroposophy had to become part of the culture in Europe. That goal has an external and an internal aspect. Externally, it means you have to become really visible in society through the actions you undertake. At that time, there were only the Rudolf Steiner Clinic in The Hague, a fairly large Waldorf school in The Hague, and smaller ones in Amsterdam, Rotterdam and Zeist. Thus, as a movement, anthroposophy was hardly visible.

With the NPI I wanted to go out into the world. That means you have to develop a vision, an anthroposophical view on social problems with which you can really do something concrete. That vision we then gradually developed. Later I described this vision in my book *The Developing Organization*.'

Again, development?
'Yes, organizational development. We introduced that word in Holland. Nowadays everyone uses it. I felt that in its development every organization crosses certain thresholds in accordance with certain laws and that it is important to be aware of those thresholds. When you don't recognize those thresholds you get distorted situations, such as a pioneer business that has outgrown itself with a pioneer in charge who makes every single decision and cannot delegate.

A company has to recognize that at a certain moment the pioneer phase is over and that then a situation has to arise in which others can also become involved in the initiatives the company takes. There are a number of symptoms that indicate it is time for a pioneer business to move into the next phase: the owner no longer knows all staff members personally, the customers have become anonymous and are now called the "market", newly introduced technology demands better qualified specialists, the family capital has become insufficient, and so on. In the middle of the fifties, business in Holland consisted primarily of such distorted pioneer companies.

The phase that has to follow this I called the phase of differentiation. For instance, in the pioneer phase, the planning, execution and control of production will still be in the hands of the same person. In the next phase, these functions have to be separated and performed more or less autonomously. Within the company, a division of duties then has to arise with separate organs and responsibilities. All the time I was working with the question along what path a company develops from one phase to the next. How do such processes happen and how can you direct them? The second phase also has its limits; a differentiated company gets stuck when the internal consultations become rigid and formal, when decisiveness and flexibility are lost by the company as a whole, when communication and coordination problems arise, and when the workers start losing their motivation.

The next threshold leads to the phase of integration. Every unit of the company, also every individual person, then stands in a meaningful, free relationship to the company as a whole. When I published my book about this in 1969 all of this seemed like utopia. But if you look around you in today's corporate world you can see that the first questions in this direction are already being asked.'

The new esoteric attitude

'At the same time as the work for the NPI, which oriented me strongly to the outside world, there was in those years a different stream, a more inward one. In 1948, Willem Zeylmans asked me if I was willing to become class reader in Amsterdam. Because this is an aspect of anthroposophy that is not generally known I have to say a few words about it.

In 1923, together with the renewal of the Anthroposophical Society, Rudolf Steiner also founded the School for Spiritual Science. In a certain sense, this school formed the heart of the anthroposophical movement. It consisted of several faculties or sections, such as an agricultural section, medical, astronomical, pedagogical, artistic sections, and so on.

Outwardly, the school had the form of a sort of university but inwardly, its purpose was a renewal of the old mysteries. The School for Spiritual Science in the Goetheanum was intended by Rudolf Steiner as a new mystery school in which it was possible to obtain insight, through exercise, into supersensible realities. Not only in a general sense, the way you can find it described in Rudolf Steiner's book *Knowledge of Higher Worlds* but also in a specific sense with the intention to apply the insights one obtains in a practical way in various professions. In a certain way, you could say that the School formed the scientific core of the anthroposophical movement.

Of course, the word science here refers to spiritual science, i.e. a science that can be practised only by people who apply themselves seriously to an inner spiritual development as the foundation of their thinking, feeling, and acting out of their will in the world.

Central in this school is the so-called General Section for Anthroposophy. To that section, Rudolf Steiner gave from early 1924 on the so-called class lessons. These are meetings with a meditative character meant directly for the development of capacities with which supersensible realities can be approached. In 1923, he had three classes in mind which represented three steps, three levels of inner development. The class lessons I mentioned were for the First Class which was started after the Christmas meeting. The next two classes were never realized.'

What is the goal of this First Class?
'The first level, the First Class, was given by Rudolf Steiner as a path that begins in the world in which we stand and ends with the encounter with our own higher spirit I. Step by step, one takes this path in the nineteen lessons given by Rudolf Steiner in 1924 of which the texts were preserved. The members of the First Class of the School for Spiritual Science follow these nineteen lessons again and again, one per month. With each succeeding cycle the experience of these meetings can become more intensive.

A few weeks before his death, Rudolf Steiner had a conversation with his Austrian friend Polzer-Hoditz. At the end of that conversation, of which Polzer-Hoditz had made notes immediately afterwards, Rudolf Steiner tells him about the class lessons in Austria: "In this school lies the seed of the future as potential. If only this were understood by the members: *as potential*. When you read the class lessons, no matter where, always remember that you are not reading a learned dissertation but that you perform a "deed", that you have to accomplish a cultic deed which can connect us with the mystery stream of all time."'

Those class lessons were also given in Holland.
'Yes, Rudolf Steiner had charged Willem Zeylmans van Emmichoven with regularly giving these steps, or lessons, in Holland for people who wanted to take the path of development of this school seriously and responsibly. Because of the difficulties in the Anthroposophical Society, these lessons were not regularly given in the thirties.

After the war, the situation in the Anthroposophical Society made it possible again for Willem Zeylmans to make a fresh beginning with this First Class in Holland; he wanted to bring a real regularity into it. He asked me in 1948 to start giving the class readings in Amsterdam. He would do it himself in The Hague, and Pieter de Haan in Zeist. In Amsterdam we finally found a good location for it in the house of the physician Frank Wijnbergh. For years and years, the class lessons were given there.

Because I was doing the class reading I had to make an intensive study of the texts delivered by Rudolf Steiner in the nineteen class lessons he had given. I had to experience the architecture of these nineteen lessons inwardly and also ask myself what the meaning of the Class is for the entire anthroposophical movement. I found the key to the answer to this question in the course given by Rudolf Steiner for young physicians just after the Christmas meeting of 1923 (*Meditative Betrachtungen und Anleitungen zur Vertiefung der Heilkunst* – JvdM).

He begins this course with the statement that the participants can consider themselves members of the School for Spiritual Science. This course, he said, is being given in the framework of the School that was just founded, and thus in the framework of the new mysteries, even though at that moment there had not yet been any class lessons. Time and again, Rudolf Steiner said after the Christmas meeting of 1923: "*Es muss ein neuer esoterischer Zug durch die Gesellschaft gehen . . .*" (A new esoteric stream needs to go through the Society – transl.) What did he mean with his new esoteric stream? I puzzled a long time about that question. No one could give me the answer. As a result of the study of the course for young physicians, but especially also in my conversations with Willem Zeylmans, I found an answer to the question.

The course presents a step by step training of physicians. The first level is described by Steiner as the exoteric level; that involves the study of anthroposophy in its entirety. In the end, that can lead to an imaginative consciousness,

59

meaning a consciousness that gains access to spiritual realities through pictures. The second level is described as the esoteric level. Inwardly, that means crossing a threshold and the things you had already understood at the first level now come back to you in a new way. A meditative deepening takes place because you start experiencing things as essential. You don't just experience the pictures in which spiritual realities clothe themselves but you start experiencing those realities more directly. In the course, Rudolf Steiner then speaks no longer of forces, of the medical effectiveness of plants and metals, but about spiritual *beings*, so-called "elemental beings" that are active in all life processes up to the high beings of the hierarchy of the angels who accompany the development of mankind.

At this second level, the question is always which beings are active in the external phenomena? Which beings manifest themselves in a plant, in a metal, in illness, but also in social phenomena? What you knew before on an imaginative level now penetrates deeper into your soul and becomes true experience. In the fourth lecture of the course, Rudolf Steiner then says: I will now stop speaking about substances but will only speak about beings.'

Which beings did he mean and how do they work in the healing process?
'In this case, we are dealing with beings from the elemental world. In old fairy tales they are called, for instance, gnomes or elves. Those beings really exist even though they are invisible to the physical eye. Beings like that are active in everything to do with life processes and, therefore, also in medicines. In matter, all sorts of beings are hidden which, in a way, are imprisoned in it and are set free through the act of potentizing. That way, these beings can have an encounter with the elemental beings which are

60

active in our metabolism and which, in our conventional science, we find described only in their biochemical effects. This biochemistry is not incorrect but it is indeed a reduction of what really takes place. For instance, what does it mean when science says that certain cells "recognize" certain substances and destroy them? Who does the recognizing and destroying? Who cures the illness?

Healing is based on encounter, the encounter of beings with each other. This generates a new development. In a therapeutic conversation it is the encounter of an I with another I, in the effect of a medical remedy it is the encounter of an elemental being with another elemental being. But what is needed then is that the remedy is "assisted" in such a way that the active beings can free themselves from their imprisonment in the substance. In anthroposophical medicine that is done by potentizing and rhythmic dilution.

Willem Zeylmans had often said in lectures that things had to find their "beingness". Through the course for young physicians by Rudolf Steiner, I began to understand what Zeylmans meant by that and, therefore, also what the significance of the First Class was. In the First Class, things are given their beingness. For myself, I have always had the following picture: in the old mysteries, you had the temple and the forecourt. On the forecourt, people could come and go, the mystery plays were held there, and the secrets of the creation of world and man were proclaimed in the form of mythological images. One could be present on the forecourt without obligation or commitment. But if you decided to participate in the real mysteries you crossed the threshold and entered the temple. Then you had to meet certain requirements. That is also the case with the First Class: it represents the temple into which you enter as a pupil.'

Your "seeing" of beings, did that also have consequences for your work for the NPI?

'Willem Zeylmans wanted to write a big book about cosmic beings, in other words, about the hierarchies, angels, archangels, archai, etcetera. But he couldn't do it alone so he formed a group of eight people among whom he divided the work. My assignment was the chapter about the activity of cosmic beings in social life. The book never made it but, in any case, as a result of all the conversations in this group, the question arose in me of how to recognize spiritual beings in everything you see in social life.'

And how do you recognize these?

'To begin with, relative to social life you must no longer think exclusively in terms of jealousy, or fear, or whatever other psychological category. You have to learn to think in terms of beings and ask yourself questions such as: which luciferic being hides behind jealousy? Which one behind pride? Which one behind untruthfulness? What is the nature of ahrimanic beings, asuric beings? (In anthroposophy, the terms luciferic, ahrimanic and asuric beings are meant to indicate different groups of beings that want to retard the development of mankind – JvdM). Those beings have no physical form and live in the supersensible world. But slowly you get the ability to pull these supersensible beings in a way to the threshold of the physical world . . .'

What does that mean: pull them to the threshold of the physical world?

'I am saying this consciously with these words, pulling the beings to the border of the visible world, because I don't want to create the impression I am clairvoyant and can behold the beings in their supersensible appearance. I can't. But I have indeed brought them to the border of visibility. They have become realities. I mean I began to live with these beings in the same way you live with realities you can see with your eyes. Only rarely have I spoken about this in public because people are shocked by it or misunderstand it.'

How do you do that, bringing these beings to the threshold of the physical world?
'For instance, you can ask the question which spiritual powers are active in world politics and with what intentions? You can go on thinking in political terms but then you never get to any real insight. Only when you begin to understand that very specific luciferic and ahrimanic beings work in the souls of people and influence the actions of those people, everywhere on earth, do you start seeing what is really happening.

The core of esotericism is not to take for granted any longer the form in which things appear but to learn to know the beingness behind those forms. You bring these beings to the border of the sense world by searching for the characteristics of their activities. For instance, luciferic beings call forth illusions, or emotions that are strongly oriented to the past. Wanting to keep things the way they have always been is a luciferic sentiment.

Ahrimanic beings, for instance, bring about soulless abstractions in thinking. Wanting to organize social life in the way you build a machine, without taking into account the unique and unpredictable elements that hide in every human being, is an ahrimanic striving. In the first step, the study of anthroposophy, you get to know the characteristics; in the second step, the really esoteric one, these become realities.'

To what extent are your actions determined by the recognition of these beings?
'After the exoteric and esoteric phases, there is a third

63

phase. Rudolf Steiner called it the *"moralische"* phase, which means acting out of esoteric insight, out of intuition. The first phase leads to imagination, the second to inspiration, and the third to intuition. In the book, *The Stages of Higher Knowledge*, Rudolf Steiner explains what he means with those concepts.

Intuition means acting on the basis of esoteric insight, or insight into the beingness of things. Of course, you can also act on the basis of external knowledge. For instance, you can study pedagogy at the Waldorf Pedagogical Academy and then apply what you learned in practice. But then, if that is all you do you work following a method. The same is true for bio-dynamic agriculture and anthroposophical medicine. If you stop in that first phase it will never get beyond applying a method. Any method can be learned, you don't need esoteric insight for that.

But acting on the basis of esoteric insight is a completely different thing. Then what is involved is not the application of a method but working on the basis of insights you have obtained on your own, insights that don't live only in your thinking but have also become realities in your feeling and willing. You decide for yourself how to act and you also know you are yourself responsible for your actions. You can no longer push this responsibility off on others, on a method, on Rudolf Steiner or anyone or anything else. You determine for yourself what is right and what is not. These choices have a moral character; that is why Rudolf Steiner calls this the *moralische* phase. The essence of the content of the First Class is that you learn to see things in their beingness, esoterically.

This is where esotericism, Rudolf Steiner's spiritual science, distinguishes itself from conventional science. In conventional science it is not admissible to ask questions about the essence, the beingness of things. What is the essence of electricity? According to the conventional view

64

that is not a valid question. You are not allowed to ask ontological questions; at most, you can ask how electricity works. Not what is warmth, but how does warmth work? In spiritual science it is exactly those questions that count.'

Did you feel a gap between this work and the work for the NPI?
'In a certain sense of course I did. Usually, I could not speak about this sort of thing with clients of the NPI but there was no need to do that. The clients had their own questions and that is what we worked with. It was not the purpose of the NPI to act as an anthroposophical missionary but to help people and organizations with their problems.

But if we got questions about the anthroposophical background of the NPI then, of course, we responded. Fortunately, that happened often. Today you can find people everywhere who are spiritually waking up. But you always have to wait until a question is asked. Willem Zeylmans van Emmichoven often said: sectarianism is giving answers to questions that were never asked! Rudolf Steiner said several times that even an initiate may not bring out anything if the world has not asked for it. By the way, everyone knew the co-workers of the NPI were anthroposophists.

There was a relation between the work for the NPI and reading the class lessons. In order to make anthroposophy part of our culture two things were necessary. On the one hand, the anthroposophical movement had to become visible in the culture and, on the other hand, more and more people in the anthroposophical movement had to start working on the basis of an esoteric attitude. That is how the right inspirations and intuitions arise. Working inwardly and outwardly at the same time, that was the point for me. The one is not possible without the other.'

65

In anthroposophical circles there has been a lot of criticism of the NPI. For instance, some people say the NPI has identified too much with business interests and has not remained faithful enough to anthroposophy.

'I know. When you act on the basis of the first level – and that happens in 99.9 per cent of all cases – you get discussions about what, from an anthroposophical point of view, is correct and what isn't. I have always felt an inner mandate to fight for the social recognition of anthroposophy. You achieve that only if you really go out into the world and help people. You can only ask for something after you have first given something. So far, I said to myself, we anthroposophists have done little more than giving lectures. Now we have to go a step further. We are going to put ourselves into a relationship with the real problems of people and see if we can help them. That means that sometimes you will do things which, in the eyes of anthroposophical theoreticians, are an abomination.

I am not interested in whether I act correctly or incorrectly from the point of view of a method. For me it is important if in a very specific, concrete situation I can do something fruitful. The good always takes place in a situation. As management consultant you get involved in the path of development of people and organizations. Then that is the important thing, not the anthroposophical truths you can proclaim. Taking the path of development of a person or an organization as the starting point, that is the road I wanted to go all those years. That does not mean I have not made mistakes. But I don't believe in unchangeable methods that are formulated somewhere in black and white.

Some anthroposophists were angry because I got involved with those "evil" business people. In their eyes business was ahrimanic. And of course that is true, in business there are strong ahrimanic forces at work. But I have always kept in mind what Rudolf Steiner once said about the destiny of captains of industry. Those people participated in a prior life in the late mysteries, in the period after 800 BC. In those mysteries these people gained enormous wisdom although this wisdom had a luciferic character. In their present incarnation, these people have to submerge themselves equally deeply in the ahrimanic in order to bring their karma into balance again. That is their destiny.

When I see one of those relatively young men, say thirty-seven years old, who runs a company of five thousand people I think: how does he do it? In such people old initiations carry over. Should we reject such a destiny on the basis of easy, methodical moralizing? Should we say: as anthroposophists we want nothing to do with that? To me that seems rather supercilious and loveless. That sort of attitude is sectarian; you close yourself off from the reality around you. You can't help another person if you don't submerge yourself in his or her destiny and experience all joy and sorrow with him or her. In today's business world there is a great deal of sorrow.'

Arriving too late, leaving too early

'In 1961, while I was still completely involved in the work for the NPI and the university, I succeeded Willem Zeylmans, after his death, as Chairman of the Anthroposophical Society In The Netherlands. He had already asked me before if I would be willing to become his successor and my answer had been: it seems to me an awful thing to do, it is almost impossible to combine with what I have to do in this phase of my life. Two tasks that are so different . . . Then he said: I know, and that's exactly why I am asking you, I follow the old Jewish proverb: give the power to those who don't long for it. Think about it, he said, but I hope you will agree to do it. I thought about it but I knew ahead of time it was inescapable. I could and would not say no to Willem Zeylmans.'

Did you have the feeling the Society accepted you as chairman?
'The majority of the members certainly did. But some smaller groups didn't at all. There were people who held it for impossible for anyone to succeed someone like Zeylmans. I had no illusions on that point.'

How did you handle that resistance?
'I didn't pay much attention to it. I saw it as my task to bring anthroposophy into the world, to root it in society. I directed myself to that task. For myself, I sought the solution to problems of this kind in humour. In addition, I can get along well with people who say openly that they disagree. Then a clear situation is created. What I have never liked is indirect resistance.

I have always striven to bring together in the work situation people with totally different insights and backgrounds. That way, what you are doing becomes fruitful.'

You were chairman until 1975. Looking back, how do you characterize your work for the Society?
'I was a transition person. I have always had that feeling: I met anthroposophy a year after Rudolf Steiner's death and I will be gone before a new great impulse will come along. Rudolf Steiner predicted that around the end of this century a new strong impulse would come from the spiritual world. I only experience the beginning of that now. It is my destiny to build a bridge between two great movements, that of the beginning and that of the end of this century.'

You came just a little too late and you leave just a little too early?
'Right.'

An open door

'In 1971, the *Vrije Hogeschool* was founded in Driebergen.
Just as with the NPI, it had an esoteric side and an exoteric
side. The exoteric one was that for ten years, at the request
of the Board of Trustees of the School of Economics in
Rotterdam, I had been its student psychiatrist. During
those ten years I gave classes one day per week and was
there for psychiatric consultation one day per week.

I was involved there with students who discovered in
their third or fourth year that they had chosen the wrong
subject. That brought them into inner problems, depres-
sions, hopelessness. There were others who hadn't a clue as
to how to get a grip on their study, even in a practical sense,
for instance, how to make a summary of a book. There were
some who copied a third of the book and then thought they
had made an excerpt of it. Then they were surprised they
failed their exams. The whole book, I repeated over and
over again, has to be summarized on one sheet of paper.
That way you get an overview.

After some time, I started classes about studying and
being a student. A thousand students in the hall! Six
months later I gave it up. Speaking with a thousand people
at the same time didn't work. Then the idea arose for a
preparatory year for undergraduate students. In the end,
that led to the establishment of such a year at the Institute of
Technology in Twente and later also in the framework of
the Vrije Hogeschool in Driebergen. It still exists.

The other aspect was that I realized we had penetrated
early childhood, grade school and high school with

69

anthroposophy, but had not yet reached the college level. We have the people, perhaps not to staff entire faculties, but certainly to make a beginning. In 1956, Zeylmans had made a beginning by starting a psychological faculty for students from Leiden and Delft despite the fact there were not enough teachers for it. It did not succeed. With that experience in the background, I did not want to do more than we could actually realize. Presently we have the situation that the Vrije Hogeschool offers a variety of graduate courses which can be viewed as the core of something larger.

Today the Vrije Hogeschool has a twenty year history behind it. When you see how many of those more than two thousand students have become active in the anthroposophical movement . . . Not that we pushed anthroposophy on them, we didn't do that, but those students woke up during that preparatory year.

We need more and more of these types of institutes where young people, who have to wage the spiritual battle at the end of this century and the beginning of the next one, can wake up. In today's education systems, there is enormous cultural and spiritual poverty. That is why first the horizon has to be broadened before these students throw themselves into an actual study. Consciousness of history, consciousness of culture, an elementary insight into the psychology of Freud, Jung and Assagioli, these are very important as fundamentals for subsequent conscious choices.'

Isn't it time after twenty years for the Vrije Hogeschool to establish some faculties?
'That door is still open. Indeed, much has changed in those twenty years. The present president, Cees Zwart, has been able to find for the faculty a number of university professors who are also anthroposophists. I believe indeed that the school is gradually coming into a new phase. The question,

of course, is what form you should give it. In addition, there is the financial problem. The whole school depends on money that is brought in each year by about one hundred and twenty students. There is no subsidy.'

Every time again you have succeeded in finding the money. For Zonnehuis, for the NPI, for the Vrije Hogeschool. And every time these were not small amounts.
'Always when I started something new, I took care of two things. First, I immediately looked for a successor.'

First?
'Yes, an initiative must never completely depend on yourself alone. Also, I always wanted to be able, in time, to withdraw to perform other tasks. When I became Chairman of the Anthroposophical Society, I also did that. I looked around me and thought: do I see anyone who will be able to succeed me in the future? That was Ate Koopmans who did indeed succeed me in 1975. A very different person than I am. But I found it really important that my successor could bring something totally different to the Society than I had done.

Besides a possible successor I also always looked for someone to whom the financial part could be entrusted. For the Vrije Hogeschool, that was Adriaan Deking Dura, who at that time still worked for the bank Mees & Hope. I told him: all you do at that bank is making money for other people, why not come and do that for us? But he had to stay there for another two years and therefore could only work for the Vrije Hogeschool in his weekends. After those two years, he and his wife Ria sold their house and took a two room apartment in the house on the Reehorst, the grounds where later the Iona Building of the school would be built. Such co-workers of the first hour often made great sacrifices, people forget that sometimes.

People complain sometimes that they cannot find the money they need for their plans. But I always say: if a plan is good, the money will surely come. The reverse is also true: if there is no money, the plan is not yet good enough and you have to find a way to discover what it is that isn't right yet. When Deking Dura said we had to wait with something or other I would say: all right, then we wait. You must be able to wait! When he said: now is the time to put down a new building, the Iona building, I said: fine, we are going to build. I have always been lucky in finding competent people who could be trusted in this respect.

I never had time for dreamers. Nor for unimaginative bookkeepers who could only tell me that something couldn't be done.'

IV. The coming spiritual struggle

In 1990, Bernard Lievegoed publishes the book *Mystery Streams of Europe and the New Mysteries* in which he describes the history of mankind as a process of differentiation. Lievegoed describes the history of mankind as a process of differentiation, and the future of mankind as a process of integration. What once was a whole fell in the course of history, and for good reasons, into many pieces. Races, cultures, religions, mystery streams, and finally also individuals became separate, even stronger: they fight each other for life and death. Against this background, Lievegoed sketches the history of mankind, the eras, the cultures; he places the various mysteries in time and describes their specific properties. Then he characterizes the European mystery streams, the eastern Grail stream, the western Celtic stream, the northern Germanic stream and the southern Rosicrucian stream. As the final one, he places Rudolf Steiner as the spiritual integrator in the heart of this European cross. During the Christmas meeting of 1923 of the Anthroposophical Society, this society, says Lievegoed, was appointed by Rudolf Steiner as the social organ in which the integration must begin to take place.

The square of time

'From the beginning, I have occupied myself in the study of anthroposophy with the qualities and the effects of the seven planets and the seven metals. I bring that theme with

73

me. My first lecture in Dornach was about the seven metals. I had only just become a member. In fact, I was so strongly oriented to sevenness that for years I could not do anything with twelveness. For instance, I could never remember the twelve signs of the zodiac and I had to learn them by heart every time again. They were not an inner reality for me.

A second theme I inwardly brought with me was the cooperation between the archangels Raphael and Michael. You know that Rudolf Steiner says the archangels "reign" in turn over successive epochs. Now it is the time of Michael. Raphael then does not stop working into mankind, only he does so indirectly, not through the innermost being of man but "through the Earth" and thus reaches the human will. That means that the spiritual impulses from Raphael's time, which preceded Michael's time, undergo a metamorphosis. To understand that, you have to examine what took place of an essential nature during this time of Raphael.

That time begins with the Grail impulse, with Parcival. Later you get the impulse of Chartres and, finally, that of the Templars. An important theme for me was to discover how these three impulses return in a different form in the present time, the time of Michael. In other words, what Michaelic form they got. While in the meantime, the continuing thread on earth, the progress of Christian esotericism, is provided by the stream that became visible in the sixteenth century under the name of the Rosicrucians.

And then you come to the question that was asked of me long ago: What in anthroposophy is really Rosicrucianism and what is truly anthroposophy? That is a very important question. From the beginning, Rudolf Steiner said repeatedly: what I bring is in essence a Rosicrucian Christianity.

In the clinic in Arlesheim I once gave a lecture about that question and said then: the relationship of Rosicrucianism to anthroposophy is as the relationship of threeness to fourness. In my experience, this is a very important theme with which people in anthroposophical circles ought to work much more. In all expressions of Rosicrucianism you always find threeness. Take for instance the well-known series of sayings: Ex Deo nascimur, In Christo morimur, Per Spiritum Sanctum reviviscimus, which mirror the Trinity of the Father, the Son and the Holy Ghost. Another threeness directly connected with the previous one is that of the body, the soul and the spirit. And out of that appears another one: thinking, feeling and willing.

Threeness always has to do with space. As soon as spirit reveals itself in space it happens in the form of threeness. The human form is threefold: spirit, soul and body. Even the form of primal rocks is threefold: feldspar, quartz and mica. Threeness arises when spirit makes itself visible in space. In the Foundation Stone which was spoken by Rudolf Steiner during the Christmas meeting of 1923 you also find this threeness: you could say the three parts stand as columns in space.

Threeness says: thus things *are*. But then suddenly, you find in the Foundation Stone a fourth element, a fourth formula completely different in rhythm and content that is added to the three great ones. The fourth formula deviates in form from the previous three. And what really happens then is that time is added to space, the development of processes through time. Steiner says in that formula:

> At the turning-point of time
> The spirit-light of the world
> Entered the stream of earthly being . . .

Something happens in time there, something becomes history.

Everything that takes place in time appears as fourness. Take for instance the development of the earth: in the first

75

phase the earth appears as Saturn, then as Sun, after that as Moon and, finally, in the fourth phase as Earth. Threeness is static and spatial and expresses: this is how things are. Fourness is dynamic, has to do with time and expresses: this is how things develop, this is how things change. All that is threeness is granted to mankind by divine powers; all that is fourness is not granted but must be gained.

Everything in anthroposophy which is based on three-ness is Rosicrucian revelation; everything which is based on fourness is anthroposophy itself, is the path of development, and that is the addition of Rudolf Steiner. He brought the path of development in time. This twoness: threeness in relation to fourness, that is the foundation of the whole of anthroposophy. All other connections, those of sevenness and twelveness, arose from the combination of threeness and fourness. The square of time connects itself with the triangle of created space.

In the threefold social order of Rudolf Steiner you have to do with a threeness, that of the life of the spirit, the life of rights and the life of the economy, that must be created by man. However, this threeness cannot be pushed over the existing realities but must be realized step by step by people who never stop searching for factual possibilities. Every social organization, be it the state or a family, must be brought into a growth process by its own members, on its way to an ideal form.

Only later did I understand that I have always rather spontaneously oriented myself toward fourness, toward development. When I started with the NPI and went deeply into Rudolf Steiner's lectures about social questions I always found threeness there: that of arranging society in accordance with the realms of spirit, rights and economy. But when I tried to understand something I concretely met in my work I arrived at fourness. That is wrong, I then thought, because in social life things have to revolve around spirit, rights and economy. Rudolf Steiner's contribution to the social question even carries the name threefoldness!

But later I understood that when Rudolf Steiner speaks about the threefoldness of the social organism he means the form, the revelation of spiritual lawfulness in space. He does not go into how you get to that form, how you realize it in actual fact. He spoke about the archetypal form, the ideal form. He discussed that the realization of the ideal form must be found in the concrete situation, by people who stand in that situation and have the necessary competence in their field.

A great Rosicrucian revelation is also that of freedom, equality and brotherhood, the slogan of the French revolution. But to realize it you must dare to go into fourness, into development in time. As soon as you dare to do that and turn away from the fatal objective of "adopting" threefoldness, come what may – as if you could force society to be suddenly threefolded from one day to the next – practical anthroposophy arises. The Rosicrucians bring the form in space, anthroposophy brings the development of that form in time.

Thus again, cooperation! To bring into a fruitful relationship that which formerly was separate, the truth of threeness and the activity of fourness. Rudolf Steiner describes this so wonderfully using the working method of the ancient mysteries in Ephesus as an example. At dusk, the teacher and the pupil walked together through the woods around the temple and observed the plants. The teacher then looked at the form of the plants, the pupil watched the streaming of the sap of the plants. Then they both went to sleep and the next morning they related their dreams to each other; during the night, the insight of the teacher in the form and the insight of the pupil in the streaming of the sap had deepened.

Through the exchange and cooperation arose the insight into the healing effect of the plant. In the mysteries of Ephesus the pupil was as important as the teacher. One studied biochemistry, the other morphology, to use modern terminology. Nowadays, morphology is not even taught any more; today's entire medicine is based on biochemistry. Man has become a bag full of biochemical processes. Because of that, insight into the qualities of threeness, in the total form of plants and man, has been completely lost.

The theme of threeness and fourness, is one of those important themes I experience as urgent and that I hope to describe in a book some day before my head rests on the pillow for the last time.'

Really, the heart of your message is always, and again now:
that which is separate and appears impossible to combine,
bring it together through cooperation.

'That could well be the essence, yes. Breaking through rigidity. A one-sided orientation towards threeness leads to inflexibility, and a one-sided orientation towards fourness to confusion and chaos. If you say, and there are people who say such things: anthroposophy is understandable only through the book *Philosophy of Freedom*, or only through Goetheanism, or only through medicine, or only through threefoldness, then rigidity arises, dogmatism. Such one-sidedness is suggested to us by Luciferic demons: my point of view is the only correct one! But note that Michael, the archangel who watches over our time as a protective angel, says that only the confluence of points of view leads to insights with which you can meet the future. Michael, as Sun Spirit, gathers up the working of all planets into one goal for the future.

During my life I have worked with fourness somewhat more than with threeness. Sometimes I have been one-sided in this and often I have had to search for balance. The central word in my life was development. You don't help an adolescent by telling him how he will or should be when he is sixty. You help someone by asking what the next little step should be. And that is: bringing threeness through fourness. It took a long time before I dared to think this way.'

What was it that you did not dare to think?
'That fourness was also right. Mostly I heard people speak about threeness: social problems are solved by threefolding! But real life demands a confluence of threeness and fourness.

Fourness involves four qualitative steps in a process of development. First, there is what you could call Saturn warmth, analogous to Rudolf Steiner's description of the evolution of the earth. In his book *Occult Science* he names the first appearance of the earth "old Saturn" and the active and creative element in that appearance was warmth. The enthusiasm for a goal, for instance, with which an initiative often begins, can be compared with this warmth.

Second, there is the light of the sun, analogous to the second appearance of the earth, "old Sun". Here comes the "enlightening" insight into how the goal can be realized. Third comes the phase that can be compared with "old Moon", that of bringing the process in motion, the approach, the action plan. And fourth is the crystallization of the goal into concrete forms. This fourth phase can be compared with the last appearance of the earth, Earth itself, characterized by solidity and physical firmness.

Enthusiasm, insight, action, and result . . . those are the successive phases of the development process of fourness. Threeness plays a role from the first phase in the enthusiasm for the goal until the last phase in guarding the realized form. Threeness provides the foundation for the entire development process.'

A Christian infrastructure

Rudolf Steiner speaks about the end of the twentieth century as a period in which a great spiritual struggle will take place. Anthroposophy, he says, has the task to play a major role in that struggle. The anthroposophical movement will have to be ready for it, otherwise the history of mankind will take a dramatic turn.

In a lecture Rudolf Steiner says that around the year 2000, the work of Lucifer, Ahriman and Michael will be so intermingled that no one will be able easily to distinguish between them. I have always understood that Rudolf Steiner meant to say: prepare yourselves for a time in which it will not be easy to get a clear aim at things. The good will not simply be recognizable as good, nor will evil as evil. In that situation, humanity will have to be able to find the eye of the needle.

The question is: how will the Luciferic forces work? In this connection, Rudolf Steiner already in the beginning of this century points to Arabism and orthodox Islam. The angel who inspired Mohammed is Lucifer. Islam has a clearly luciferic character; a complex and extensive system of rules and regulations determines from the outside how people should behave. People are not addressed in their individual conscience. Just like the Old Testament, the Koran contains a great many rules for the outer life.

Undoubtedly, and this is how I have seen it since 1950, there will be an orthodox reawakening of Islam at the end of the century. Already now you can see the first beginnings of it, primarily in Iran, but also in other Islamic countries. In view of the understandable emotions that live in those countries it is not unthinkable that this reawakening will end up in a new Holy War. The development of those countries has been very fast. When Rudolf Steiner spoke in the beginning of the century about these developments there was not much happening yet in those countries. Even in 1950, oil did not yet play a decisive role in the world economy. That only happened because of the expanding culture of affluence that arose in the West after 1950. Iran with its Shah did not amount to much in the world, and there were endless numbers of separate sheikdoms that were rarely heard of.

Then we had the phenomenon of the Moslems who started to come to the West – just like a thousand years before when they came with entire armies and were beaten back at Poitiers in France. When they started coming to Holland as foreign workers at the end of the fifties and into the sixties of this century I had to think of my father who always said about the employment of coolies on the island of Sumatra: this is an unallowable form of economic slavery for which we will have to pay dearly. At the end of the fifties, I said that openly at an annual meeting of the Central Social Employers Association. I had the feeling that the importation of cheap labour from the Islamic countries was a form of economic slavery. These days it tends to be forgotten that we have lured those people to Europe ourselves.

Little by little, the oil sheiks got more and more power. In fact, financially and economically speaking, they have already conquered Europe. Just look at how many companies and large projects in the West are financed with oil dollars. Millions of Europeans today work in the service of Arab oil sheiks.

After that came the ayatollahs, Khomeiny in the lead, but that is still no more than a beginning. The climax is yet to come, around the year 2000 and after. How will it go? I don't know but the outline is clear: the West will come more and more into the grip of orthodox Islam. And we don't need to have any illusions about the motivations of orthodox Moslems. Just look at someone like Khomeiny who was guided by the most dangerous illusions. Also look at Saddam Hussein who during the war with Iran sent millions of Iraqis into senseless death. And look what he did in Kuwait. What did he achieve with it? Nothing at all. That is an important luciferic characteristic: the pursuit of illusions, even to death.

Then there is the question as to how the Ahrimanic demons work. On a worldwide level, Rudolf Steiner said, Ahriman works through the Mars demons, the negative side of the activity of Mars. The Mars point on earth lies in the area of Outer Mongolia and northern China. In the history of China you can see that these Mars demons become active every eight hundred years and activate the Mongolian tribes. China built its Great Wall against these recurring incursions. The latest great Mongolian periods of reawakening extended their influence into Europe, namely in the years from 350 to 450 and from 1150 to 1250 AD. The next period runs from 1950 to 2050 and we are smack in the middle of it. In 1924, in a conversation with young people in Breslau, Rudolf Steiner said that quieter times will not come until after the year 2050.

The historic attacks of the Mongols in Europe always had an abrupt end because of the appearance of a Christian initiate. In the year 450 such a sudden end took place in front of Rome when Attila had a meeting with Pope Leo II. Around 1250, after the battle of Liegnitz, a similar thing happened when the grandson of Jengis Khan came under the influence of Saint Hedwig.

According to Rudolf Steiner, the deeper tension in the world lies between China and America. He predicted that the tension between East and West, that between Russia and the United States, would cease to exist and that gradually another, deeper one would become visible between China and America. When in 1917 the Bolshevists came to power in Russia he said: they will not be able to keep their hold of Russia for more than seventy years. And that is exactly what has happened! We have all grown up with the idea that world politics were determined and dominated by the contrast between capitalism and communism. Those were the great enemies facing each other and no one could imagine that it would ever change. But Rudolf Steiner saw immediately that this great polarity would one day end and change into a different enmity that will prove to be much more essential and dangerous.

Lucifer works through pride, fundamentalism, illusion; Ahriman works through power and cold hate. The idea has risen in me that it is the task of the anthroposophical movement to build a Christian infrastructure in the world. Just as Saint Hedwig, Elisabeth of Thueringen's aunt, did for the area around Liegnitz. She founded monasteries and convents, started schools, and invited Cistercians to Silesia to bring the wilderness under cultivation and begin agriculture. With such activities the entire spiritual aura of a region changes. The Mars demons, called anti-Michael demons by Rudolf Steiner, become aware of the Christian light in the aura, flee and leave the armed forces behind in consternation. All the soldiers can do is to go home as quickly as they can.

With the word *Christian* I do not mean Christianity in the sense in which the word is used in churches, for there fundamentalism can also live. With the word *Christian* I mean a society that takes into account the spiritual origin and future of every individual, a society on the basis of individual responsibility and freedom. You might think of a large number of small anchor points in our culture, such as a school in a city, a shop in a village.

How can people become convinced that they are not powerless, that they do not say: what can I do all by myself? What is important is not the quantity but the quality, what happens that is really essential. Because of all those small anchor points the etheric world changes. World history is not determined by physical power relationships but by spiritual qualities.

Earlier, we dealt with the three levels, the exoteric, the esoteric, and the "moral". When you start acting from the second level, i.e. based on insight into beings hidden behind external appearances, the quantitative effect of the action is no longer important but its qualitative effect is. In silence, you can help change things. A small Christian anchor point in a city changes something in the aura of that city.

At the second level in a way, you stand between Lucifer and Ahriman. In this way, Rudolf Steiner portrayed in a great sculpture created for the interior of the first Goetheanum, and saved because at the time of the fire it had not yet been installed, the figure of Christ standing between Lucifer and Ahriman. Lucifer makes souls unfree by harassing them with feelings of pride and illusory thoughts, Ahriman does this by inspiring them with a cold, calculating spirit and hate. Christ makes inner freedom possible, a narrow line between Lucifer and Ahriman. In our time, no one thinks any more of living adversary powers, of demons, but it is so incredibly important to do just that. The same is true for thinking about Christ. Exoterically, Christ is no more than a tradition, a legend, a beautiful story that can warm hearts or leave them cold. Esoterically, however, he is a being, a reality, a cosmic identity you can meet inwardly and with whom you can work.

Inner life, that is what counts in the end. Whatever you do in the world, if it is not based on real inner life, on a concrete experience of spiritual realities, then it doesn't amount to much. Even if, from the outside, it looks as if you have achieved a lot. And that inner life must not be based on feelings of duty, the idea that you call yourself an anthroposophist and therefore you have to meditate. It must really be based on an inner necessity. If you do it out of duty Lucifer has got you. He loves to see you inwardly squirm, that you struggle with all the things that don't succeed and that you are burdened by the secret questions whether you really are mature enough, spiritual enough. Think of all the anthroposophists in this century who have tried to do the exercises described by Rudolf Steiner in his book *Knowledge of Higher Worlds*. And how many of them, if they were honest, have not had to admit falling short in that regard?'

Do you mean that book is no longer right for this time?
'Already in 1920 Rudolf Steiner asked Maria Roeschl, the leader of the Youth Section of the School for Spiritual Science, to rewrite that book, among other things, for the young people. At that time already, he thought it did not have the right form any more for young people, that the *form* was antiquated, not the *content*. Life did not permit her to accomplish this task.'

In what way is the form antiquated?
'Rudolf Steiner never distanced himself from the content of the book. That has always remained valid. For people who want to reach insight into higher worlds it is indispensable. However, after 1923, its form became antiquated. After all, the book was written in the beginning of this century in the language of the older theosophists of that time. You really have to know that to understand the book properly.
   In the book, which Rudolf Steiner wrote as a series of articles in 1904 and 1905, and which he thoroughly reworked in 1914, he describes the so-called "Moon way".

To understand that designation, you should read the lectures he gave in England in August 1924 that are published with the title *True and False Paths in Spiritual Investigation*. In essence, the Moon way involves a way towards insight into spiritual realities that begins with thinking and then leads upward, step by step, through the imaginative and inspirational capacities, to the untuitive capacity.

Only in 1924, less than a year before his death, he speaks about a different way towards insight into higher worlds, the so-called "Saturn way". This way is exactly the reverse; it starts with intuition, then leads via inspiration, and ends with imagination. You can also call it the social way; it connects with what people do, to put it better perhaps, it begins with an action you take based on an intuition. The starting point is not the imaginative life as it is in the Moon way but the life of action.

Rudolf Steiner had prepared this new way from about 1910. In the end, he formulates the spiritual task of the anthroposophical way in the lecture he gave on December 31, 1922, the evening of the fire of the first Goetheanum. In brief, the content of that lecture is as follows: All the old mysteries were *wisdom* mysteries; those mysteries were about the knowledge given by the gods about the creation of the cosmos and man. In the sacred cult of the Christian churches, that path of revelation is followed further with the sacrifice of Christ on Golgatha as its center. Whoever inwardly experiences this cult receives the gifts the divine powers grant to mankind. Besides this path, Rudolf Steiner describes a new path that can be walked in the present time under the guidance of the archangel Michael, the way of the *reverse cult*. Here it is not the divine hierarchies that address themselves to man but man who addresses the hierarchies. Man offers the fruits of his spiritual striving, acquired through the resistance presented by the world, to the hierarchies. The School for Spiritual Science, founded a year after this lecture, is based on this reverse cult. The essence is then no longer the acquisition of wisdom but doing the good.

Also the Foundation Stone I mentioned before, which Rudolf Steiner gave during the Christmas meeting in 1923, is based on the reverse cult. The fourth and last part ends with the following lines:

> That good may become
> What from our hearts we would found
> And from our heads direct
> With single purpose.

That good may become what we, human beings, can contribute to the evolution of the earth and the cosmos . . . In essence, this second way is connected with the lectures Rudolf Steiner gave in those years about karma and reincarnation. Karma also has a revealing, passive side and an active side that is directed to the future. Karma is not only passively letting the consequences of your actions in prior lives come over you but also taking deliberate actions towards the future. Where karmic consequences of the past are concerned the spiritual powers are active, but where the future is concerned man must become active himself.'

A mercurial person

'Karma exists only between people. Personally, an individual has no karma. But an individual does have a karmic relationship with nature, with people. Karma is always enacted between two realities, between one person and another, between a person and a group of people, between a group and another group. A month after the Christmas meeting of 1923, Rudolf Steiner begins to speak about karma and he continues with it until he dies of illness in September 1924. (See *Karmic Relationships* – JvdM) In those lectures, the subject is always the relationship of someone to something or someone else through the relationship you have to things, because of events and experiences in prior lives. You can change that relationship in the present life by taking hold of things in a certain way. Then you make karma into the future. Old karma Steiner calls Moon karma, new karma he calls Sun karma, the karma you create in this life.'

To what extent did the content of those lectures relate to the new esoteric attitude Rudolf Steiner spoke about after 1923?
'He began to speak about karma in a totally new way! Formerly, karma was fate. And now karma became freedom! Karma gives you in freedom the possibility to change your relationship to things. By adding new elements to it, elements you choose yourself. No longer is it only the deeds of the gods, the old sisters of fate, that determine your destiny. You can take your destiny in your own hands.

Earlier, in 1912, he had already tried to speak about karma in that new way. But then that was not yet possible; his lectures then generated such powerful emotions with his audience that he had to stop them. In those days, thinking about karma and reincarnation was still strongly determined by the theosophical approach. I heard a story once that there was a café in Munich frequented by the theosophists. On one wall there was a row of pictures with portraits of famous personalities of the past, on the other wall a row of portraits of members of the Theosophical Society who frequented the café. The "initiated ones" knew then that theosophist X was an incarnation of the famous personality portrayed in the picture straight opposite the portrait of X. Rudolf Steiner called that *Unfug*, nonsense.

But for the members, that was proof of being a high initiate: knowing who you were in a previous life. Knowing his karma was for him the most important thing. Who is who . . . Much more important, however, is the question: how has the former personality, who is now dead and does not exist any more, *metamorphosed itself* in its life between death and new birth? What is its new task? And how do the karmic influences from the past carry over into the present life? Questions like that make dealing with karma into something concrete, something that is fruitful for new things.

If I resolve, to put it popularly, between death and new birth to learn something very specific in the coming life, then that resolution determines my life. To a group of young people Rudolf Steiner said once You should ask yourself the question: to what stream do you belong? That is important. That way you know your internal sources and goals, and also where you are one-sided, where you have to complete yourself. Destiny only becomes fate when it has to manifest itself violently to you; as soon as you accept your destiny, however, it creates the possibility to add something to it in freedom. Then it becomes a gift you can use for something new.

The Saturn way begins with the question: how can I work out of the life of the will, the life of action, out of what I want to *become?* That can only happen in a karmic relationship, it doesn't matter to what. This does not mean you should only work with people you belong to, whom you experience as your "pals". No, you also have karmic relationships to people you experience as your enemies. The question is: in that karma, how can you accomplish something? That is only possible by doing something, by performing a deed. You act on the basis of an intuition and then you look in all inner quiet at what the effect is of the action.

This involves a conscious action. Unconscious actions never come from a clear intuition, but from some stimulus out of the past. Suppose you have a difficult relationship with someone. If in all inner peace you decide to cooperate with that person, simply because you recognize that the person objectively has something to do with the project you want to undertake, no matter how different his ideas about it may be from yours, then tremendous power can emanate from that decision. I have seen that more than once. Based on that inner resolution, you perform a conscious deed in the direction of that person.'

Such as?
'For instance, you approach someone like that and you say: I know we don't like each other, that we would like nothing better than to be in each other's way as much as possible. But for the business, wouldn't it be better for us to accept each other? Such a gesture, provided it is based on the real will to cooperate with the other, can bring about miracles. It can even result in close friendships. And nothing is so fascinating as a friendship with someone who is totally different from yourself.

From 1923 on, Rudolf Steiner described karma in such a way that you understood: no longer do the gods exclusively determine your life, you can also do something about that yourself. Actually, he formulated karma so as to bring it in accordance with the intentions of the Archangel Michael who, as we know, waits until in freedom man performs a deed. Only after that deed is done Michael comes to help. He undertakes nothing out of himself but waits until man does something. What does this mean? It means you have to learn to observe the consequences of your actions. That is the essence of the Saturn way: perform a deed and then wait. It is the archetypal picture of creation: God created the world and saw that it was good. None other than the Creator himself went the Saturn way!'

What Rudolf Steiner calls the Saturn way has to do with the reverse cult he describes in the night of the fire of 1922-23.

Does karma play no role when we go the Moon way?
'The Moon way you can go all alone. You can lock yourself into your study and start with the exercises Rudolf Steiner describes in *Knowledge of Higher Worlds*. You don't need anyone else for that, at least not in the beginning. In the end of course, you also arrive at a deed. But on the Saturn way you start with that right away. That's why it makes no sense to look for that way in your study. You won't find it there. Outside in the street, at work, in intensive relationships with people, that's where the Saturn way lies.

The young people of those days, different from the older members, wanted to do something with anthroposophy. They wanted to found schools, start farms, set up medical institutes, etcetera. They wanted to live anthroposophy in their hands and feet, in their will, in the resistance of their actions. That is why Rudolf Steiner started speaking to that group about the Saturn way. That way is appropriate for people who want to live an active life. The older ones were angry about that. They said to Steiner: these young people want to start a school and they have only just become members of the Society; they don't have any wisdom yet. Steiner would then reply: if you are honest in what you want to do the spiritual world accepts your enthusiasm for wisdom.

How could you dare to do anything before you had meditated on the content of the book *Theosophy* at least twelve times? Only then have you achieved a foundation for action! That is how many older members thought in those days. Every self-respecting anthroposophist at that time had a special meditation space in which he spent an average of two hours per day. In their daily life they did not notice anything of those meditations. That was not allowed. Daily life had to be strictly separated from the inner way. Daily life was the bad world, you had to make a living there. The real higher life consisted of your experiences in your study. For those people it was really awful that Rudolf Steiner suddenly threw himself into the social question and developed the threefold idea. Social threefolding was for them a beautiful thought you certainly should not try to put into practice.

Everything can degenerate, also the Moon way. I have heard people say: Doing something isn't possible yet, the world isn't ready for that. Threefolding? Perhaps in five hundred years when people have made some substantial progress. For now, we as anthroposophists have the task to think these things through. Above all, we should not do anything because then things will go wrong. Doing something in this bad world always means that it ends up in failure. Actually, anthroposophy is too beautiful, too true, too good for this world.

It is true that something must be thought through before anything can happen. That is the great importance of the Moon way. But people with a lot of willpower cannot wait till they are sixty and mature enough to start doing something. Rudolf Steiner's complaint was always: only after they have retired are anthroposophists ready to start doing something.

Later in my life I had an experience that taught me something else. As a physician, I was called to an old woman who was ill in bed, an anthroposophist of the very first hour. In all respects, she had led an inconspicuous life. Only in the final stage of her life, her spiritual greatness was manifested. An indescribable light surrounded her. In that experience I learned that also such quiet, meditating people change the world!'

'I am a mercurial person. I wake up through the things that happen, the things I experience in groups, the work I do. When by myself, I am not very creative, in contrast to someone like Willem Zeylmans who was most creative when he was alone and much less so when working as part of a group. The Moon way, to be honest about it, has always given me problems. I have always diligently tried to do the exercises but it continued to be a laborious business. I have learned through doing. Whenever there is nothing I can do any more I lose grip of my inner development. That is why I am so happy with the courses I may teach every year to the first year students at the Vrije Hogeschool. There I experience every time again how true it is that the Michaelites, the Michaelic souls are coming to earth now.

They are present everywhere, in former East Germany, in Hungary, Czechoslovakia. Take someone like Havel, his *Letters to Olga* . . . Havel is also a man who learns through action. This Saturn way, it is so hard to talk about it exactly because it is a way you have to go by taking action. But if you have an eye for it, all around you see the people who seek that way, to take direct action. For that, you need to have the courage to jump into the water and learn to swim in the process.'

Afterword
by Bernard Lievegoed

Little has been said and much has remained unmentioned. May I make an effort to summarize it all?

Youth
The karmic choice to incarnate in the tropics brought with it the formation of a mobile etheric body. The multicultural environment provided a foundation for my interest in people with varying backgrounds.

The encounter with my parents and educators gradually gave me the self-confidence which by nature, and because of an illness in my youth, was not strong.

As a whole, it was an ideal preparation for the life I had to lead later on. The whole has made my external biography possible.

Inner biography
This is characterized by a late awakening. For a long time, I led a life of fantasy in solitude, on the one hand oriented towards technical fantasy, on the other hand towards questions about the *being* of man. Where does man come from? How does he function? What and who am I?

The inner biography became possible because of the connection with the School for Spiritual Science (membership of the First Class). From 1932 on, I have tried to go that path, 42 years as class reader and teacher. This means that I was permitted to go this path with a group of people 21 times in a two-year cycle. A path that does not seek more wisdom but lays the foundation for action on the basis of the reverse cult. No study path but the path of a cult that goes further, step by step.

In view of my age, I have transferred this task and now I may continue as a regular participant. I have learned that this path really exists only if people in fact walk it or, better said, if it is created anew every time again.

Just as an institute for higher education, this school is a public one. People who register for it must satisfy some minimal prerequisites just as is the case with every other education program.

A second theme in the inner biography was to choose certain fields of interest and to work at those for many years. There is, for example, the subject of the qualities of the planets. For more than twenty years, I occupied myself with thse. Then there is the time of Raphael in the Middle Ages, the three great spiritual movements of the grail (with Parcival), the School of Chartres, and the Templars. In all of this, the metaporphosis of the Raphael time into the Michael time was central. Finally, the problems of psychiatry and psycho-therapy have coloured everything.

By nature, I am a speaker, not an author. My father was primarily an author and when he spoke he used a langauge that could be printed right away. The publications that nevertheless came from my hand consist of written lectures most of which were given many times from different points of view and for a variety of audiences. In the end, these lectures were condensed into a written test in which the traces of the spoken word could still clearly be found.

These are some systematic aspects of my inner biography. The ups and downs of that biography remain a personal matter.

My biography was unthinkable without the warm relations with many friends. In the interview, Willem Zeylmans van Emmichoven and Ita Wegman are mentioned, and also Herbert Hahan who lived in *Zonnehuis* for seven years. I also have to mention the physicians in the clinic in Arlesheim, especially Dr. Margarete Bockholt and Dr. Stavenhage (later Frau Dr. Hauschka). With Eugen Kolisko, also mentioned in the interview, I had intensive contacts for a long time as I did with other immediate co-workers of Rudolf Steiner.

I would have been unable to accomplish my external biography without the support and confidence of my wife, in Zonnehuis known as Dr. Nel Schatborn, with whom I managed Zonnehuis in the beginning. After 1954, I was able to assume my duties at the NPI because she, together with a group of trusted Zonnehuis co-workers, further developed curative education in the Netherlands.

She too has always found her strength in working together with people, with me for 56 years now. My life has been blessed because, with every initiative, there were always people who connected themselves with it and who were able to continue and develop the work autonomously.

At my age, you experience the following. As soon as you let yourself go a little and you notice what comes up from the unconscious you are presented with pictures from your life you had long forgotten.

Often these are pictures of situations in which things did not succeed, because at that moment you failed to respond in the right way. For instance, you remember a conversation of fifty years ago in which you did not react to what someone said or asked, in which you sent the person away empty-handed because you were tired or preoccupied, or you were irritated. These are the sins of omission Rudolf Steiner spoke about and that weigh most heavily in our life among people. And you start to experience: exactly these, seemingly unimportant events, form the basis for your coming personal karma.

Zeist, 1991

Bibliography

Books by Bernard Lievegoed

Maat, ritme, melodie. Grondslagen voor een therapeutisch vebruik van muzikale elementen, Zeist 1983
Phases of Childhood, Floris, Edinburgh 1987
The Developing Organization, Blackwell, Oxford 1991
Phases, Rudolf Steiner Press, London 1979
Towards the 21st Century, Doing the Good, Toronto 1972
Samenwerkingsvormen, Zeist 1988
Man on the Threshold: The Challenge of Inner Development, Hawthorn Press, Stroud 1985
Lezingen en Essays 1953-1986, Zeist 1987
Mystery Streams of Europe & the New Mysteries, Atnthroposophic Press, New York 1982

Other books referred to in the text

Margarete and Erich Kirchner-Bockholt, *Rudolf Steiner's Mission and Ita Wegman*, Privately printed, London 1977
Vaclav Havel, *Letters to Olga*, Faber, London 1989
Rudolf Steiner:
Karmic Relationships, Volumes 1-8 (GA 235-240, 1924)
Rudolf Steiner, *Karmic Relationships Vols 1-8* (London, variously 1971-1989)
The Philosphy of Spiritual Activity, Rudolf Steiner Press, Bristol 1992
The Guardian of the Threshold (in *The Four Mystery Plays*, RSP, London 1982)

True and False Paths in Spiritual Investigation, RSP, London 1985

Theosophy, RSP, London 1989

The Stages of Higher Knowledge, Anthroposophic Press, Hudson, New York 1993

Knowledge of the Higher Worlds: How is it Achieved? RSP, Bristol 1993

Occult Science: An Outline, RSP, London 1984

Rudolf Steiner & Ita Wegman, *Fundamentals of Therapy* RSP, London 1983

Bernard Lievegoed's* last book provisionally titled

Concerning the Saving of the Soul

will be published in Spring 1994
by Hawthorn Press

*Born on 2nd September 1905, Sumatra;
Died on 12 December, 1992, Zeist, Holland.

Books from Hawthorn Press

DEVELOPING COMMUNITIES

Bernard C. J. Lievegoed
comprising
FORMING CURATIVE COMMUNITIES
translated by Steve Briault
CONCERNING ORGANIZATIONS OF THE SPIRITUAL LIFE
translated by Simon Blaxland de Lange
Forming Curative Communities addresses the development of all forms of communities and groups that come into existence with a spiritual/cultural aim. The author discusses the dynamics that evolve, and emphasizes the 'moral technique' to ensure real success of the community.
Concerning Organizations of the Spiritual Life offers further insights and directions about community living. Lievegoed suggests approaches to working together and staff training methods that will truly help people to work together.
217 × 138mm; 224 pp;
sewn limp bound;
ISBN 1 869 890 30 2

MAN ON THE THRESHOLD

Bernard C. J. Lievegoed
Humanity is crossing a major threshold. Boundaries that formerly surrounded human life are no longer fixed. The theme of *Man on the Threshold* is inner development. During the course of the book a practical outline of an anthroposophiclal approach to inner training and development unfolds. Professor Lievegoed is a distinguished physician, educator and industrial psychologist, and he was awarded the *Golden Quill* literary award from the Netherlands Publishers' Association following publication of this book, owing to his significant contribution to Dutch cultural life. The book is compelling, and urges readers to put into practice what they have read.
210 × 134mm; 224 pp; paperback;
ISBN 0 950 706 26 4

COPING WITH KARMA
Joop van Dam
Recognizing your life's path
tranlsated by Jakob M. Cornelis

This book explains how to develop a conscious
awareness of one's destiny, one's karma, by the means
of certain exercises and attitudes. It becomes possible
to recognize the self-laid path and to realize that
whatever happens always embodies the potential for
development.
217 × 138mm; 64 pp; paperback;
ISBN 1 869 890 33 7

LIFE PATTERNS
Jerry Schöttelndreier
**Responding to life's questions, crises and
challenges**
translated by Jakob M. Corenelis

Life Patterns offers a method that enables individuals
to take stock of their present life situation, to
understand their roots, to gain practical and spiritual
insights into their own personal setting, and to
consider the way ahead.
217 × 138mm; 64pp; paperback;
ISBN 1 869 890 27 2

SOULWAYS
Rudolf Treichler
translated by Anna Meuss
**The developing soul – life phases, thresholds
and biography**

Soulways offers insights into personal growth through
the phases and turing points of human life. A
profound picture of child and adult development is
given, including the developmental needs, potentials
and questions of each stage. Drawing on his work as a
psychiatrist, Rudolf Treichler also explores the
developmental disorders of soul life – additions,
neuroses, hysteria, anorexia, schizophrenia and others.
Soulways is a valuable guide for professionals and lay
people interested in personal growth.
210 × 135mm; 320 pp; sewn limp bound;
ISBN 1 869 890 13 2

THE TWELVE SENSES
Albert Soesman
translated by Jakob Corelis
The senses both nourish our experience and act as
windows on the world. But overstimulation may
undermine healthy sense experiences. The author
provides a lively look at the senses, not merely the
normal five senses, but twelve: touch,, life, self-
movement, balance, smell, taste, vision, temperature,
hearing, language, the conceptual and the ego senses.
The imaginative approach provides an accessible study
guide for teachers, doctors, therapists, counsellors,
psychologists and scientists.
210 × 135mm; 176 pp; sewn limp bound
ISBN 1 869 890 22 1

RUDOLF STEINER
Rudi Lissau
An introduction
This book gives a vivid picture of Rudolf Steiner's life
and work. It aims to point out the relevance of
Steiner's activities to contemporary social and human
concerns. Different chapters look at Steiner's
philosophy; his view of the universe, earth and the
human being; Christ and human destiny; the
meditative path; education and social development;
approaches and obstacles to Rudolf Steiner's work.
210 x 135 mm; 192 pp; sewn limp bound
ISBN 1 869 890 06 8

102

If you have difficulties ordering from a bookshop
you can order direct from Hawthorn Press
1 Lansdown Lane, Lansdown, Stroud, Glos.
United Kingdom GL5 1BJ

Telephone 0453 757040   Fax 0453 757040